D1405734

WORLD OF ANIMALS

# 39

# FISH

## SPINY-FINNED FISH 1

Sticklebacks, Sea Horses, Gurnards, Flounders ...

JOHN DAWES

an imprint of

**■SCHOLASTIC**

www.scholastic.com/librarypublishing

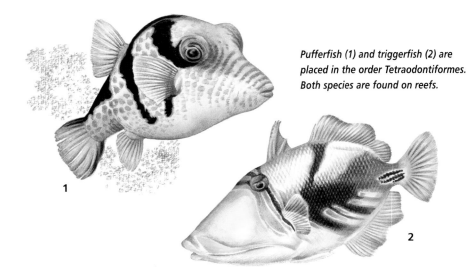

*Pufferfish (1) and triggerfish (2) are placed in the order Tetraodontiformes. Both species are found on reefs.*

1

2

Library of Congress Cataloging-in-Publication Data

Fish.
    p. cm. - - (World of Animals)
    Contents: vol. 31. Primitive fish -- vol. 32. Sharks -- vol. 33. Rays, chimaeras, and eels -- vol. 34. Carps, minnows, and allies -- vol. 35. Salmon, trout, and allies -- vol. 36. Cod, herring, and allies -- vol. 37. Catfish -- vol. 38. Piranhas -- vol. 39. Spiny-finned fish 1 -- vol. 40. Spiny-finned fish 2.
    ISBN 0-7172-5905-6 (set: alk. paper) -- ISBN 0-7172-5906-4 (vol. 31) -- ISBN 0-7172-5907-2 (vol. 32) --ISBN 0-7172-5908-0 (vol. 33) -- ISBN 0-7172-5909-9 (vol. 34) -- ISBN 0-7172-5910-2 (vol. 35) -- ISBN 0-7172-5911-0 (vol. 36) -- ISBN 0-7172-5912-9 (vol. 37) -- ISBN 0-7172-5913-7 (vol. 38) -- ISBN 0-7172-5914-5 (vol. 39) -- ISBN 0-7172-5915-3 (vol. 40)
    1. Fishes--Juvenile literature. I. Grolier (Firm) II. World of animals (Danbury, Conn.)

QL617.2.F55 2004
597--dc22

2004047333

Published 2005 by Grolier, an imprint of Scholastic Library Publishing Danbury, CT 06816

This edition published exclusively for the school and library market

**The Brown Reference Group plc.**
(incorporating Andromeda Oxford Limited)
8 Chapel Place
Rivington Street
London EC2A 3DQ

© 2005 The Brown Reference Group plc.

**Project Directors:**     Graham Bateman, Lindsey Lowe
**Editors:**               Marion Dent, Andrew Stilwell,
                           John Woodward
**Art Editor and Designer:**     Tony Truscott
**Picture Managers:**      Helen Simm, Becky Cox
**Picture Researcher:**    Alison Floyd
**Main Artists:**          Denys Ovenden, Mick Loates,
                           Colin Newman
**Indexers:**              Michael and Marion Dent
**Production:**      Alastair Gourlay, Maggie Copeland

Printed in Singapore

Set ISBN 0-7172-5905-6

# About This Volume

**A** sea horse looks nothing like a flatfish. Indeed, a sea horse does not look like a fish at all. The flatfish, for its part, begins life like a "normal" fish but ends up living on the bottom, lying on its right side or its left side with both eyes on the same side of its head. A fangtooth has teeth to match its name and lives in permanent darkness at water depths of 16,400 feet (5,000 m), while a stickleback lives in streams and ditches and sticks its nest together with a secretion from its kidneys. A stonefish has such a venomous sting it can kill a human in a few hours, and the shrimp fish lives its life standing on its head. Appearances can be deceptive, though, for despite their obvious differences, these fish, along with 12,100 others, share several features that link them together. The most significant feature is the presence of spines on the fins, especially the dorsal (back), anal (belly) and pelvic (hip) fins. This single characteristic is responsible for the collective name given to the whole group: the spiny-finned fish (series Percomorpha). There are so many species in the series, with such interesting lifestyles, shapes, and sizes to describe, that both this volume and Volume 40 in this set of books are devoted to the hugely varied and often spectacular spiny-finned fish.

# Contents

*The Chinese trumpetfish lives on Indo-Pacific coral reefs, where it feeds on fish and shrimp.*

*The banded yellowfish (1) catches small prey with its pincerlike jaws, while the common fangtooth (2) uses its huge mouth to engulf anything it can.*

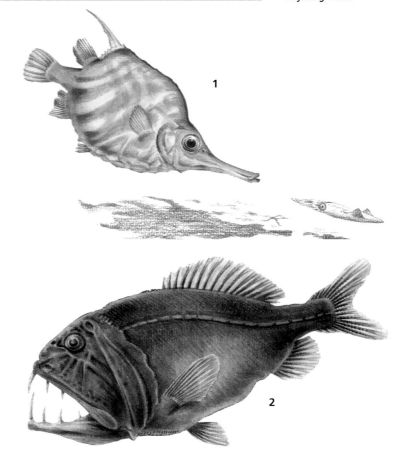

# How to Use This Set

**W**orld of Animals: Fish is a 10-volume set that describes in detail fish from all around the world. Each volume features species that are grouped together because they share similar characteristics. So all the world's sharks are found in Volume 32, carplike fish are in Volume 34, catfish are in Volume 37, and so on. To help you find the volumes containing species that interest you, look at pages 6 and 7 (Find the Animal). A brief introduction to each volume is also given on page 2 (About This Volume).

## Data panel presents basic statistics of fish or fish group

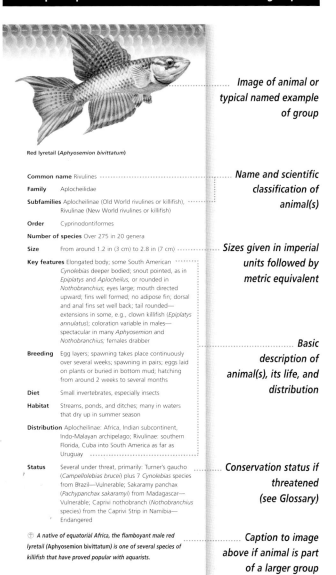

Red lyretail (*Aphyosemion bivittatum*)

**Common name** Rivulines ............ *Name and scientific classification of animal(s)*

**Family** Aplocheilidae

**Subfamilies** Aplocheilinae (Old World rivulines or killifish), Rivulinae (New World rivulines or killifish)

**Order** Cyprinodontiformes

**Number of species** Over 275 in 20 genera

**Size** From around 1.2 in (3 cm) to 2.8 in (7 cm) ........... *Sizes given in imperial units followed by metric equivalent*

**Key features** Elongated body; some South American *Cynolebias* deeper bodied; snout pointed, as in *Epiplatys* and *Aplocheilus*, or rounded in *Nothobranchius*; eyes large; mouth directed upward; fins well formed; no adipose fin; dorsal and anal fins set well back; tail rounded—extensions in some, e.g., clown killifish (*Epiplatys annulatus*); coloration variable in males—spectacular in many *Aphyosemion* and *Nothobranchius*; females drabber

**Breeding** Egg layers; spawning takes place continuously over several weeks; spawning in pairs; eggs laid on plants or buried in bottom mud; hatching from around 2 weeks to several months ........... *Basic description of animal(s), its life, and distribution*

**Diet** Small invertebrates, especially insects

**Habitat** Streams, ponds, and ditches; many in waters that dry up in summer season

**Distribution** Aplocheilinae: Africa, Indian subcontinent, Indo-Malayan archipelago; Rivulinae: southern Florida, Cuba into South America as far as Uruguay

**Status** Several under threat, primarily: Turner's gaucho (*Campellolebias brucei*) plus 7 *Cynolebias* species from Brazil—Vulnerable; Sakaramy panchax (*Pachypanchax sakaramyi*) from Madagascar—Vulnerable; Caprivi nothobranch (*Nothobranchius* species) from the Caprivi Strip in Namibia—Endangered ........... *Conservation status if threatened (see Glossary)*

*A native of equatorial Africa, the flamboyant male red lyretail (*Aphyosemion bivittatum*) is one of several species of killifish that have proved popular with aquarists.* ........... *Caption to image above if animal is part of a larger group*

........... *Image of animal or typical named example of group*

## Article Styles

Each volume contains two types of article. The first kind introduces major groups of fish (such as the ray-finned fish or the perchlike fish). This article reviews the variety of fish in the groups as well as their relationship with other groups of fish. The second type of article makes up most of each volume. It concentrates on describing in detail individual fish, such as the thornback ray, families of fish, such as hammerhead sharks, or groups of related families. Each such article starts with a fact-filled **data panel** to help you gather information at a glance. Used together, the two styles of article enable you to become familiar with specific fish in the context of their evolutionary history and biological relationships.

## Article describes a particular fish or group of fish

*Scientific name of animal*

*Common name of animal*

*Captions to photographs provide additional information about each animal's lifestyle*

SHARKS

# Gray Reef Shark

*Carcharhinus amblyrhynchos*

Like many other animals, the gray reef shark sends out unmistakable visual messages when it feels threatened. If these signals are ignored, the shark may attack with devastating consequences.

WHEN THREATENED, MANY ANIMALS EXPERIENCE A RUSH of adrenalin that prepares them to attack or flee. In such a situation sharks like the gray reef shark send out an unmistakable warning message to those around them. We ignore such powerful "fight or flight" signals at our peril.

**Common name** Gray reef shark (long-nosed blacktail shark)

**Scientific name** Carcharhinus amblyrhynchos

**Family** Carcharhinidae

**Order** Carcharhiniformes

**Size** Up to 8.4 ft (2.6 m) but usually smaller

**Key features** Sleek, dark-gray or bronze-gray back fading to white on the underside; long snout with underslung mouth; caudal fin has distinct black edge (hence one of the shark's common names); some individuals have white-tipped first dorsal fin (they are regarded as *C. wheeleri* by some authorities)

**Threat and Attack**

The gray reef shark is not among the largest of sharks, neither is it indiscriminately aggressive. It is, nonetheless, one of the species most frequently implicated in attacks on humans. That is not because the shark actively seeks out an unsuspecting victim to attack. It is because the species appears to define a territory around itself—a "personal space"—and reacts quite forcefully if it feels it is being threatened.

For this reason divers that encounter this wide-ranging shark are advised not to approach it rapidly, not to get too close, and not to startle it by sudden movements or noises. In any of these situations many other sharks would take flight. However, the gray reef shark will often not just stand its ground but will go into a characteristic series of body movements that leaves the observer or intruder in no doubt that the shark feels threatened.

If the intruder persists, it is likely that the display will intensify, culminating sooner or later in an attack. However, if the messages being sent out by the shark are read and understood, and a careful retreat is made, the risk of attack subsides. The shark may also retreat once it no longer feels threatened.

It appears that such encounters occur with greater frequency when a lone gray reef shark

**Breeding** Internal fertilization; embryos develop a placenta through which they obtain nourishment for up to 1 year; 1–6 pups produced in a latter

**Diet** Wide range of bony fish, as well as squid, octopuses, lobsters, and crabs

**Habitat** On continental and island shelves and on coral reefs, preferring deeper waters around the dropoff zone (where the reef plunges sharply at its ocean-facing edge); also found in atoll passes and in shallower areas with strong currents

**Distribution** Widely distributed in tropical zones of both the Pacific and Indian Oceans; if *C. wheeleri* is accepted as being a variant of *C. amblyrhynchos* rather than a separate species, then the range extends into the Red Sea and down as far as South Africa

**World population** Abundant at many locations within its range, but may be declining in some areas

*Scientific name of animal*

*Common name of animal*

SEE ALSO Sharks, Ground 32:42

*Cross-references to relevant pages in this and other volumes*

*Easy-to-read and comprehensive text*

A number of other features help you navigate through the volumes and present you with helpful extra information. At the bottom of many pages are **cross-references** to other articles of interest. They may be to related fish, fish that live in similar places, fish with similar behavior, predators (or prey), and much more. Each volume also contains a **Set Index** to the complete *World of Animals: Fish*. Most fish mentioned in the text are indexed by common and scientific names, and many topics are also covered. There is also a **Glossary** that will help you if there are words in the text that you do not fully understand. Each volume includes a list of useful **Further Reading and Websites** that help you take your research further. On page 7 you will find a complete checklist of all the fish superclasses, classes, and orders of the world and where they are featured in the set.

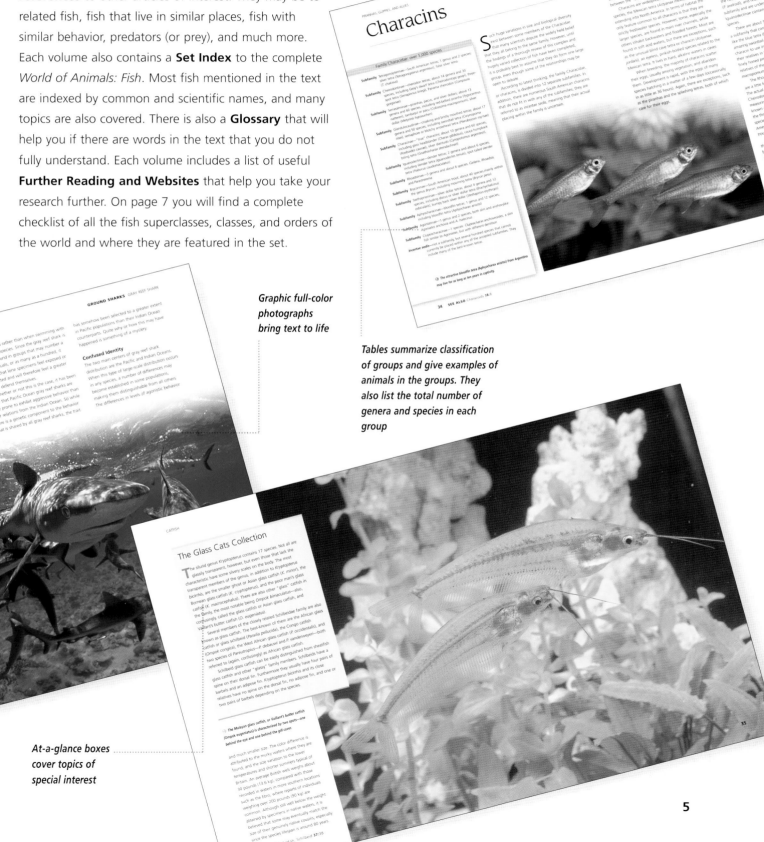

*Graphic full-color photographs bring text to life*

*Tables summarize classification of groups and give examples of animals in the groups. They also list the total number of genera and species in each group*

*At-a-glance boxes cover topics of special interest*

# Find the Animal

**W**orld of Animals: Fish is the fourth part of a library that describes all groups of living animals. Each cluster of volumes in World of Animals covers a familiar group of animals—mammals, birds, reptiles, amphibians, fish, and insects and other invertebrates. These groups also represent categories of animals recognized by scientists (see The Animal Kingdom below).

| Rank | Scientific name | Common name |
|---|---|---|
| Phylum | Chordata | Animals with a backbone |
| Superclass | Gnathostomata | Jawed fish |
| Class | Actinopterygii | Ray-finned fish |
| Order | Characiformes | Characoids |
| Family | Characidae | Characins |
| Genus | *Pygocentrus* | Piranhas |
| Species | *natereri* | Red-bellied piranha |

## The Animal Kingdom

The living world is divided into five kingdoms, one of which (kingdom Animalia) is the main subject of the World of Animals. Kingdom Animalia is divided into numerous major groups called phyla, but only one of them (Chordata) contains animals that have a backbone. Chordates, or vertebrates, include animals like mammals, birds, reptiles, amphibians, and fish. There are about 38,000 species of vertebrates, while the phyla that contain animals without backbones (so-called invertebrates, like insects and spiders) include at least 1 million species. To find which set of volumes in the World of Animals you need to choose, see the chart below.

## Fish in Particular

World of Animals: Fish provides a broad survey of some of the most abundant, unusual, varied, and yet rarely seen creatures on our planet. Fish are unique among vertebrates because all species live in water—although some have adapted to spend periods on land. Fish are

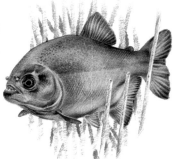

*The kingdom Animalia is subdivided into groups such as classes, families, genera, and species. Above is the classification of the red-bellied piranha.*

divided into major groups called superclasses, classes, and orders. The two superclasses comprise the jawless and the jawed fish. Different classes include fish such as lobe-finned fish, cartilaginous fish, and ray-finned fish. In each class there are often a number of fish orders, and in the orders there are families. All the fish superclasses, classes, and orders are shown on page 7; the common names of some of the most important species in these groups are also listed.

Fish classification is a changing science. Not only have several different ways of grouping fish already been proposed, but new evidence, such as from DNA analysis, has resulted in a major rethinking of the fish family tree;

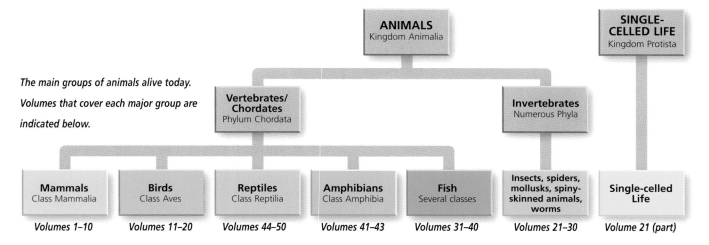

*The main groups of animals alive today. Volumes that cover each major group are indicated below.*

| | | | | | | |
|---|---|---|---|---|---|---|
| **Mammals** Class Mammalia | **Birds** Class Aves | **Reptiles** Class Reptilia | **Amphibians** Class Amphibia | **Fish** Several classes | **Insects, spiders, mollusks, spiny-skinned animals, worms** | **Single-celled Life** |
| Volumes 1–10 | Volumes 11–20 | Volumes 44–50 | Volumes 41–43 | Volumes 31–40 | Volumes 21–30 | Volume 21 (part) |

ANIMALS
Kingdom Animalia

SINGLE-CELLED LIFE
Kingdom Protista

Vertebrates/Chordates
Phylum Chordata

Invertebrates
Numerous Phyla

the result is that some species are now placed in different groups by different scientists. Furthermore, the same fish may have a different name under different systems of classification. Therefore the system of classification in this set may differ from others and may itself change as the results of new studies emerge. The system followed mostly here is the one devised by Joseph S. Nelson in *Fishes of the World* (John Wiley & Sons, Inc., 1994).

## Naming Fish

To discuss animals, names are needed for the different kinds. Red-bellied piranhas are one kind of fish and black-spot piranhas another. All red-bellied piranhas look alike, breed together, and produce young like themselves. This distinction corresponds closely to the zoologists' definition of a species. All red-bellied piranhas belong to one species, and all black-spot piranhas belong to another species.

Most animals have different names in different languages. Therefore zoologists use an internationally recognized system for naming species consisting of two-word scientific names, usually in Latin or Greek. The red-bellied piranha is called *Pygocentrus natereri* and the black-spot piranha *Pygocentrus cariba*. *Pygocentrus* is the name of the genus (a group of very similar species) that includes red-bellied and black-spot piranhas; *natereri* or *cariba* indicates the species in the genus. The same scientific names are recognized the world over. This allows for precision and helps avoid confusion. However, a species may have more than one scientific name—it may have been described and named at different times without the zoologists realizing it was one species.

## FISH SUPERCLASSES, CLASSES, AND ORDERS

| | |
|---|---|
| **SUPERCLASS AGNATHA** | **jawless fish** |
| Order Petromyzontiformes **(Vol. 31)** | lampreys |
| Order Myxiniformes **(Vol. 31)** | hagfish |
| | |
| **SUPERCLASS GNATHOSTOMATA** | **jawed fish** |
| | |
| **CLASS CHONDRICHTHYES** | **cartilaginous fish** |
| Order Heterodontiformes **(Vol. 32)** | bullhead sharks |
| Order Orectolobiformes **(Vol. 32)** | carpet sharks |
| Order Carcharhiniformes **(Vol. 32)** | ground sharks |
| Order Lamniformes **(Vol. 32)** | mackerel sharks |
| Order Hexanchiformes **(Vol. 32)** | frilled and cow sharks |
| Order Squaliformes **(Vol. 32)** | dogfish sharks |
| Order Squatiniformes **(Vol. 32)** | angel sharks |
| Order Pristiophoriformes **(Vol. 32)** | saw sharks |
| Order Rajiformes **(Vol. 33)** | rays |
| Order Chimaeriformes **(Vol. 33)** | chimaeras |
| | |
| **CLASS SARCOPTERYGII** | **lobe-finned fish** |
| Order Coelacanthiformes **(Vol. 31)** | coelacanths |
| Order Ceratodontiformes **(Vol. 31)** | Australian lungfish |
| Order Lepidosirenifomes **(Vol. 31)** | South American and African lungfish |
| | |
| **CLASS ACTINOPTERYGII** | **ray-finned fish** |
| Order Polypteriformes **(Vol. 31)** | bichirs and ropefish |
| Order Acipenseriformes **(Vol. 31)** | sturgeons and paddlefish |
| Order Amiiformes **(Vol. 31)** | bowfin |
| Order Semionotiformes **(Vol. 31)** | garfish |
| Order Osteoglossiformes **(Vol. 31)** | bonytongues and allies |
| Order Elopiformes **(Vol. 31)** | tarpons |
| Order Albuliformes **(Vol. 33)** | spiny eels |
| Order Anguilliformes **(Vol. 33)** | eels |
| Order Saccopharyngiformes **(Vol. 33)** | swallow and gulper eels |
| Order Clupeiformes **(Vol. 36)** | herring and allies |
| Order Cypriniformes **(Vol. 34)** | carp and minnows |
| Order Characiformes **(Vol. 38)** | characins and allies |
| Order Siluriformes **(Vol. 37)** | catfish |
| Order Gymnotiformes **(Vol. 33)** | New World knifefish |
| Order Esociformes **(Vol. 35)** | pikes, pickerels, and mudminnows |
| Order Osmeriformes **(Vol. 35)** | smelts and allies |
| Order Salmoniformes **(Vol. 35)** | salmon, trout, and allies |
| Order Stomiiformes **(Vol. 35)** | dragonfish and allies |
| Order Ateleopodiformes **(Vol. 35)** | jellynose fish |
| Order Aulopiformes **(Vol. 35)** | lizardfish |
| Order Myctophiformes **(Vol. 35)** | lanternfish |
| Order Lampridiformes **(Vol. 35)** | oarfish |
| Order Polymixiiformes **(Vol. 35)** | beardfish |
| Order Percopsiformes **(Vol. 36)** | trout-perches and allies |
| Order Ophidiiformes **(Vol. 36)** | cusk eels and brotulas |
| Order Gadiformes **(Vol. 36)** | cod and allies |
| Order Batrachoidiformes **(Vol. 36)** | toadfish |
| Order Lophiiformes **(Vol. 36)** | anglerfish and allies |
| Order Mugiliformes **(Vol. 38)** | mullets |
| Order Atheriniformes **(Vol. 38)** | rainbowfish and silversides |
| Order Beloniformes **(Vol. 38)** | flying fish and ricefish |
| Order Cyprinodontiformes **(Vol. 38)** | piranhas, guppies, and allies |
| Order Stephanoberyciformes **(Vol. 39)** | pricklefish and allies |
| Order Beryciformes **(Vol. 39)** | fangtooths and allies |
| Order Zeiformes **(Vol. 39)** | dories and allies |
| Order Gasterosteiformes **(Vol. 39)** | sticklebacks, sea horses, and allies |
| Order Synbranchiformes **(Vol. 33)** | swamp eels and allies |
| Order Mastacembeliformes **(Vol. 33)** | spiny eels |
| Order Scorpaeniformes **(Vol. 39)** | mail-cheeked fish |
| Order Perciformes **(Vol. 40)** | perchlike fish |
| Order Pleuronectiformes **(Vol. 39)** | flatfish |
| Order Tetraodontiformes **(Vol. 39)** | triggers, puffers, and allies |

# SPINY-FINNED FISH

**D**eep in the cold, dark waters of the world's oceans live fish that few people have ever seen, dead or alive. Among them is a superefficient, small hunter—the fangtooth (*Anoplogaster cornuta*)—with teeth that match its name. In the freshwater rift lakes of Africa live a bewildering array of colorful, mouthbrooding cichlids (family Cichlidae) that look nothing like the fangtooth. Yet remarkably they are related.

⬇ *Picasso triggerfish* (Rhinecanthus aculeatus), *in the family Balistidae, have an extraordinary locking mechanism on their fin spines that they can use to lodge themselves inside a crevice, from which it is almost impossible to remove them.*

## First and Second Impressions

At first sight there appear to be no similarities between an African mouthbrooder and a fang-toothed, deep-sea hunter that can spend its entire life in permanent darkness at depths of as much as 16,400 feet (5,000 m). Just as there does not appear to be any similarity between an inoffensive, elegant sea horse (family Syngnathidae) that does not even look or swim like a fish and a stonefish (family Scorpaenidae) whose venom can kill a human in an hour or two. But look more closely, and similarities begin to become apparent—so similar that they must all be related to each other, whether distantly or closely.

Some of the features linking all these diverse groups together are only found when an internal examination of the skeleton and some organs is carried out.

For example, the position of the pelvic and pectoral fins is very similar in all these fish (though not all have pelvic fins). In the vast majority of species that do, the pelvics are located either in the chest or throat (thoracic or jugular), while the pectorals are placed high on the side of the body and close to the back edge of the head.

Most significantly, there are spines on the fins, especially the dorsal, anal, and pelvics. It is this that has given the common name to the whole spiny-finned fish series—Percomorpha. However, these three external features are not the only ones that percomorph, or spiny-finned, fish share. They also have a protractile upper jaw that can be extended forward, a valuable asset when hunting. They also have pharyngeal teeth on the upper and lower sections of the throat part of the mouth.

Most species have ctenoid scales in which the back (exposed) edge is covered in small teeth (ctenii), although some have cycloid scales that do not carry the teeth along the back edge. Most species also have well-developed eyes, but they can be quite small in some types—for example, the deepwater flabby whalefish (family Cetomimidae).

Not every species, genus, or even family will have all the above external features, let alone the internal ones relating to skeleton and organs. Nevertheless, every major group will have a sufficient number, particularly of spines on the fins, to identify them as members of the series Percomorpha. In total, the series has ten orders, with around 226 families, around 2,150 genera, and over 12,100 species (numbers vary depending on classifications).

### Pricklefish and Relatives

This order (Stephanoberyciformes) is predominantly deepwater fish, but little is known about some of them. Despite being predators, these fish do not have large

## Who's Who among the Spiny-finned Fish?

**Series** Percomorpha—10 orders
   **Order** Stephanoberyciformes—9 families and over 80 species; pricklefish and relatives
   **Order** Beryciformes—7 families and over 154 species; fangtooth and relatives
   **Order** Zeiformes—6 families and about 44 species; dories and relatives
   **Order** Gasterosteiformes—10 families and about 316 species; sticklebacks and relatives
   **Order** Scorpaeniformes—25 families and around 1,326 species; mail-cheeked fish
   **Order** Pleuronectiformes—11 families and over 693 species; flatfish
   **Order** Tetraodontiformes—9 families and around 410 species; triggerfish, puffers, and relatives
   **Order** Synbranchiformes—swamp eels and relatives (*see* Vol. 33)
   **Order** Mastacembeliformes—spiny eels (*see* Vol. 33)
   **Order** Perciformes—perches, cichlids, and relatives (*see* Vol. 40)

NOTE THE ABOVE DIVISIONS ARE MOSTLY BASED ON NELSON 1994 (*SEE* BIBLIOGRAPHY). SOME ALTERNATIVE CLASSIFICATIONS EXIST, AND THEY ARE HIGHLIGHTED AND DISCUSSED AT RELEVANT POINTS IN THE TEXT. NUMBERS OF SUBORDERS, FAMILIES, GENERA, AND SPECIES VARY BETWEEN CLASSIFICATIONS. WHENEVER POSSIBLE, THESE VARIATIONS HAVE BEEN TAKEN INTO ACCOUNT.

pointed teeth like other deepwater hunters. Most have large mouths, and one group (tapetails or ribbonbearers, subfamily Eutaeniophorinae) have large noses. Others, like the flabby whalefish, have very loose skin.

### Fangtooth and Relatives

The fangtooth is also a deepwater hunter and has teeth to match its name. Along with the members of six other families, the three fangtooths ("tooths" not "teeth") make up the order Beryciformes.

Among them are two families that carry light-producing bacteria in special pouches—the flashlight or lanterneye fish (family Anomalopidae) and the pineapple and pinecone fish (family Monocentridae). Some members of other families—for example, some slimeheads or roughies (family Trachichthyidae)—can also generate light, but this is done within the body of the fish rather than by the action of bacteria. The squirrelfish and soldierfish (family Holocentridae) do not generate luminescence of any kind, but they too belong to this order.

### Dories and Relatives

The John Dory (*Zeus faber*) looks gentle and inoffensive until it opens its mouth. It is absolutely huge, and as in all members of its family (Zeidae), this fish can shoot its mouth out at such speed that few prey animals escape.

# Swamp Eels, Perches, Cichlids, and Allies

This volume deals with seven of the ten orders in the series Percomorpha, the spiny-finned fish, or percomorphs. The three notable absentees—Perciformes, Synbranchiformes, and Mastacembeliformes—are discussed in other volumes:

• The swamp eels and their relatives (two orders, two families) are included in Volume 33. It has a substantial section dedicated to all types of eels, including the most famous—the European and American eels (*Anguilla anguilla* and *A. rostrata*). Thus for entries not just on swamp eels (order Synbranchiformes) but also on spiny eels (order Mastacembeliformes) refer to Volume 33.

• The cichlids (family Cichlidae), along with the various perches (families such as Percidae and Moronidae), basses (families include Serranidae and Acropomatidae), angelfish and butterflyfish (families Pomacanthidae and Chaetodontidae), wrasses (family Labridae), gobies (family Gobiidae), tunas and mackerels (family Scombridae), swordfish and marlins (families Xiphiidae and Istiophoridae), plus a large number of other species (around 9,300), are discussed in Volume 40, which is dedicated exclusively to the order Perciformes.

The John Dory and its closest relatives are also exceptionally thin for their size and therefore can almost disappear from view as they drift deceptively innocently toward their victims. Other members of the order are not so thin, although they all have the large, pointed heads and mouths that are typical of the dories.

Among these members are the boarfish (family Caproidae) and the oreos (family Oreosomatidae), making up a total of around 44 species in the order Zeiformes.

## Sticklebacks and Relatives

The sticklebacks and their allies account for about 316 species, making up the order Gasterosteiformes. Some of the characteristics shared by many representatives include platelike scales (scutes) on the body and a pointed snout that is almost tubelike in some species.

While the dorsal, anal, and pelvic fins contain strong spines in many species, perhaps most notably in the sticklebacks themselves (family Gasterosteidae), other members of this order lack the strong spines, as well as some of the fins. The best examples of this latter type are the sea horses (family Syngnathidae).

The unusual tubesnouts (family Aulorhynchidae) and equally unusual "winged" seamoths (family Pegasidae), along with the controversial paradox fish (*Indostomus paradoxus*, family Indostomidae), are also members of this order. So are the superficially similar trumpetfish

(family Aulostomidae) and cornetfish (family Fistulariidae), along with their own closest relations, the snipefish (family Macramphosidae) and the remarkable shrimpfish (family Centriscidae)—some can dive with lightning speed among the long, venomous spines of sea urchins and also spend much of their lives standing on their heads.

## Scorpionfish and Relatives

This order, Scorpaeniformes, contains the world's most venomous fish—the stonefish; some can cause an excruciatingly painful death in just one hour. Together with the scorpionfish they form the family Scorpaenidae. Some authorities separate the two types, along with some others, into distinct families, so the total number of families and subfamilies in this order can vary considerably depending on whose classification is being followed.

However, there is one characteristic on which everyone agrees—it is just one bone (the "stay")—but one present in all species. It stretches from below the eye, across the cheek, to the bone lying in front of the gill cover. All members of the order share this small but significant characteristic. As a result, fish that look as different as gurnards (family Triglidae), velvetfish (families like Caracanthidae and Aploactinidae), pigfish, horsefish, or racehorses (family Congiopodidae), flatheads (families like Bembridae and Platycephalidae), the sculpins (Cottidae), greenlings (Hexagrammidae), and several

others all belong to the order Scorpaeniformes (also called the mail-cheeked fish).

## Flatfish and Relatives

The 693 or so flatfish are the most asymmetrical fish known to science. They begin life as normal symmetrical larvae, but very soon one eye begins to move. It migrates over the top of the head and comes to lie on the other side. Flatfish therefore end up with both eyes on the same side of the head. In some species the right eye moves, in others, the left; in other species the migrating eye can be either the right one or the left one—ending up with families like the lefteye flounders (Bothidae) and the righteye flounders (Pleuronectidae).

About 11 families, 123 genera, and around 693 species are recognized in this order—Pleuronectiformes—which includes halibut, plaice, sole, and their relatives.

## Puffers and Relatives

Puffers (families include Tetraodontidae), along with triggerfish (family Balistidae), boxfish (family Ostraciidae), filefish (family Monacanthidae), and gigantic molas or ocean sunfish (family Molidae), make up the order Tetraodontiformes, which contains around 410 species in about 107 genera. Triggerfish and filefish have an odd locking mechanism in their fin spines so they can lodge themselves in a crevice and cannot be dislodged.

The boxfish and their relatives do not have this special adaptation. However, they do have their bodies encased in a box or "trunk"—hence their name—which gives them a high degree of protection. Some of these fish can also produce toxins when they are alarmed to discourage any predator that sees them as a potential meal.

The puffers add a "novel" approach to self-defense—they can inflate themselves into a globe that is difficult for any predator to handle. The porcupinefish (family Diodontidae) take this ability a critical stage further by having stiff spines that cover the body.

However, the molas do not need any of these "tricks" because they can grow to 6.6 feet (2 m) and weigh over 2,200 pounds (1,000 kg). At that size they are safe from all but the largest hunters in the open seas, such as some of the oceangoing sharks.

⊖ *This bizarre-looking weedy seadragon* (Phyllopteryx taeniolatus) *from the coastal waters of New South Wales in Australia uses its fins to disguise itself among the seaweed fronds.*

**Pricklefish (*Acanthochaenus luetkenii*)**

**Common name** Pricklefish and relatives

**Families** Stephanoberycidae (pricklefish), Melamphaidae (bigscales or ridgeheads), Cetomimidae (flabby whalefish), Barbourisiidae (red or velvet whalefish), Rondeletiidae (redmouth or orangemouth whalefish)

**Order** Stephanoberyciformes

**Number of species** Stephanoberycidae: 3 in 3 genera; Melamphaidae: about 38 in 5 genera; Cetomimidae, Barbourisiidae, and Rondeletiidae: 23 in about 11 genera

**Size** From around 0.8–1 in (2.1–2.5 cm) to about 15.8 in (40 cm)

**Key features** All elongated; head blunt (pricklefish and bigscales), longer-snouted (whalefish); mouth large to very large; eyes very small (flabby whalefish), larger in others; body covered in prickly scales (pricklefish), large scales (bigscales); skin: spiny (red or velvet whalefish), scaleless or smooth in others, or very loose (flabby whalefish: has very pronounced lateral line); dorsal and anal fins sit well back (whalefish), further forward in all others; pelvic fins absent (flabby whalefish); coloration: often brown to black; red, or velvet, whalefish is bright red

**Breeding** Few details available; bigscales reportedly scatter eggs and sperm; eggs and larvae are planktonic

**Diet** Mainly invertebrates and other fish

**Habitat** Mostly deepwater marine fish; may extend into shallow water during larval stages or within any given 24-hour period; all strictly marine, some occurring at great depths

**Distribution** Worldwide but mainly in Atlantic, Indian, and Pacific Oceans

ⓐ *The 5-inch (13-cm) pricklefish (Acanthochaenus luetkenii) lives at depths from 5,430 to 17,415 feet (1,655–5,308 m). It has an immense range from the northwest Atlantic into the Indian and Pacific Oceans.*

# Pricklefish and Relatives

Stephanoberycidae, Melamphaidae, Cetomimidae, Barbourisiidae, Rondeletiidae

*Pricklefish and their closest relatives have so far eluded scientists. In most cases we know nothing of the lifestyle of these enigmatic deepwater fish.*

OVER 64 SPECIES MAKE UP FIVE of the major families in the order Stephanoberyciformes: Stephanoberycidae, Melamphaidae, Cetomimidae, Barbourisiidae, and Rondeletiidae. They include a bizarre assortment of contrasting characteristics— such as prickles and scales to no scales and smooth skin.

## Prickly Mystery

The pricklefish (*Acanthochaenus luetkenii*) is the best-known member of its small family of three species—Stephanoberycidae. We know that it occurs in the Atlantic, Indian, and western Pacific Oceans at least, because specimens have been collected from these regions. Also, these specimens were caught at depths of between 5,430 and 17,415 feet (1,655–5,308 m).

The maximum length of the species appears to be a little over 5 inches (13 cm). There is a large eye and large mouth, but no teeth on the palate (roof of the mouth). Since there are no seaweeds to feed on at such depths, this indicates that a pricklefish is a hunter of the deep. Its body is covered in prickly scales (hence the name for both the species and the family). We also know how many fins it has and how many spines and rays they contain.

As for its life history, we know absolutely nothing about it. Does it live in midwater or at or near the bottom? Does it lay eggs? If it does, does it look after them and the larvae? Does it live a solitary life, or does it live in shoals? What does it feed on? How does it catch its prey? Indeed, we are totally ignorant about all the various facets of its life—a life that is lived in total darkness and at enormous pressures.

## Better-known Bigscales

We are considerably better informed about the close relatives of the pricklefish—the bigscale fish or ridgeheads (family Megalamphaidae)—but even so, our knowledge is very limited.

It is known that there are about 38 species of bigscale in five genera. Like the pricklefish, the bigscale fish are deepwater species. The huge-mouthed yawning (*Poromitra oscitans*), for example, can be found at depths of around 16,400 feet (5,000 m); and while it is the deepest-living member of the family, others also extend to great depths. However, the upper range for many species takes them into relatively shallow water. It is from these fish that we have been able to gain some important details about their lifestyle.

For instance, some species are egg layers; they produce floating eggs and larvae that live among, and feed on, plankton. Among them is *Poromitra megalops*—a 2.5-inch (6.2-cm) species that is distributed in tropical latitudes of the Atlantic, Indian, and Pacific Oceans at depths of between 490 and 3,280 feet (150–1,000 m). *Megalops* means "large eye," which is most appropriate for this species, since its eyes are over one-fifth the length of its large-mouthed head.

In the highsnout melamphid (*Melamphaes lugubris*) the head of the planktonic larvae is duckbill-shaped; it eventually develops into the high-snouted head of the adult. This species grows to a little over 3.4 inches (8.5 cm) and is found around Japan and from the Gulf of Alaska down to the northern parts of Baja California in Mexico at depths from 165 to 3,940 feet (50–1,200 m).

The crested bigscale (*P. crassiceps*) is another egg-laying species that has planktonic eggs and larvae. It is distributed worldwide at depths of between 1,970 and 10,825 feet (600–3,300 m), except in the Arctic and the

Mediterranean; as its name indicates, it has a saw-edged crest on top of its head. At just over 7 inches (18 cm) long it is also the largest member in its family.

The smallest bigscale is "the" bigscale itself—(*Melamphaes danae*)—a tiny fish that probably does not grow any larger than 0.8 to 1 inch (2.1–2.5 cm) in length.

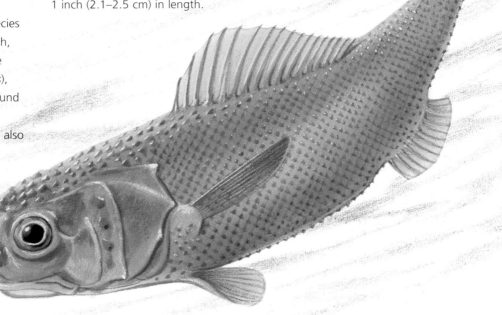

## Red and Flabby Whalefish

The whalefish were so named because they look like whales. Perhaps that is so, but you will need quite a vivid imagination to appreciate the likeness. Besides, the largest of the whalefish only grows to about 15.8 inches (40 cm).

As its name states, the red whalefish (*Barbousia rufa*) is red or reddish-orange throughout its body. Its fins and body are covered all over with tiny spines (spinules) that give it a velvety feel—therefore it also known as the velvet whalefish.

It is the largest of the whalefish and is distributed in all tropical and temperate areas of the world's oceans. Like many deepwater hunters, it has a huge mouth, and in typical whalefish fashion its dorsal and anal fins are set well back on the body. The red whalefish is also the sole representative of the family Barbourisiidae.

⬆ **Melamphaes simus** *is a member of the family of bigscale fish, or ridgeheads. It is a deepwater species found in the eastern north Atlantic.*

The redmouth or orangemouth whalefish (family Rondeletiidae) fare a little better in numbers of species; there are two in the family—*Rondeletia bicolor* and *R. loricata*. These whalefish are much smaller than the red whalefish, only growing to around 6 inches (15 cm) in length. The skin is scaleless and very smooth, but it is not velvety. As in their relatives, both species have the very large mouths that are typical of so many deep-sea predators.

There are about 20 flabby whalefish (family Cetomimidae), ranging in size from around 2.4 inches (6 cm) long, as in *Danacetichthys galatheus*, to about 12.5 inches (32 cm) in "the" flabby whalefish itself (*Gyrinomimus grahami*). These fish are called "flabby" because they have no scales, and their skin fits loosely over the muscles. They also lack pelvic fins and ribs.

Some of these 20 species are little known, although they may well be widely distributed around the world. In fact, only five species are sufficiently well known to have common names. The least known of all the flabby whalefish is *Procetichthys kreffti*; the only details come from a single specimen that was collected in a net that had been lowered to 7,217 feet (2,200 m). Whether this depth is typical or not for this species is among the many features of its biology that are still unknown.

## Other Pricklefish Relatives

There are five other types of predator that are related to the pricklefish, bigscales, and whalefish.

At a length of only 1.3 inches (3 cm) the siphonophorefish (*Kasidoron edom*) is a tiny fish

⊕ *Although the redmouth whalefish (Rondeletia loricata) is only 6 in (15 cm) long, it has the large mouth that is typical of so many deep-sea predators.*

# Big Mouth of the Deep

Flabby whalefish have immense mouths for their size. Perhaps the best example of this is *Cetomionus picklei*, a species that (like *Procetichthys kreffti*) is only known from a single, dark brown specimen. It had a Standard Length of just 2.2 inches (5.6 cm) and was collected at a depth of 6,119 feet (1,856 m) off Cape Town in South Africa. The mouth is almost impossibly large with a long lower jaw that can be extended to take in prey, which is probably as large as this flabby whalefish itself.

Living in the deepest parts of the world's oceans, where sizable prey is hard to find, many of the predators that live here have a huge mouth that allows them to attack and attempt to swallow whatever they come across, even if the intended victim is as large as the attacker itself.

with bizarre pelvic fins that split into numerous branches from base to tip, giving them a treelike appearance. This feature is so unusual that the siphonophorefish was placed in its own family—the Kasidoridae—until it was realized that it was the larval form of a gibberfish (*Gibberichthys pumilus*). Therefore the family Kasidoridae and species, *K. edom*, no longer exist. However, the family Gibberichthyidae does; it contains just two species, whose adults are found at depths of between 1,310 and 3,280 feet (400–1,000 m).

The family Hispidoberycidae contains a single species—the bristlyskin (*Hispidoberyx ambagiosus*)—that occurs at depths between 1,900 and 3,350 feet (580–1,020m). It has spiny scales, as indicated in its common name, and it also has a huge mouth. Only a few specimens have ever been collected.

The hairyfish (*Mirapinna esau*) is known from a single specimen caught close to the surface off the Azores, in the eastern Atlantic, and measured 2.2 inches (5.5 cm) in length; it had extraordinary winglike pelvic fins and hairlike growths on its body. Both the pelvic fins and the tail had extended rays. The mouth was small, and the stomach contained copepods

(tiny single-eyed crustaceans that form part of the plankton). The hairyfish is placed in its own subfamily, the Mirapinninae.

Together with five species of tapetails or ribbonbearers (subfamily Eutaeniophorinae) the hairyfish forms the family Mirapinnidae. The festive ribbonfish (*Eutaeniophorus festivus*) is long and ribbonlike (as indicated by its name). This species grows to around 2.1 inches (5.3 cm) in length and has been seen hovering vertically in the water. It is known to feed on copepods; it is also an egglayer that spawns throughout the year. In addition, the festive ribbonfish has planktonic larvae that are eel-like in appearance.

The other species are thicker-bodied and look a little more like the hairyfish. However, very little is known about them. Although some have been caught near the surface, others, such as *Parataeniophorus gulosus*, have been netted at depth—in this case, around 4,595 feet (1,400 m).

Young tapetails have a long ribbonlike extension on their tails that decreases as the fish grow. However, since all the specimens collected so far have been immature, we still know next to nothing about the biology of the adult members of this family.

## Where Are the Female Largenoses?

The largenose fish (family Megalomycteridae) consist of a group of five to seven species in three or four genera. Their most easily observed characteristic (contained in their name) is an exceptionally large olfactory (smelling) organ. Like their closest relatives, largenose fish are poorly known.

Intriguingly, all the specimens that have been examined to date are males. Where are the females? Do they occur at different depths than those at which the males have been collected? Or have they already been collected and are stored somewhere among the sample jars of fish that are waiting to be described? Or have the females already been described, but the connection with the male largenoses been missed inexplicably?

**Common fangtooth (*Anoplogaster cornuta*)**

**Common name** Fangtooths and relatives

**Families** Anoplogastridae (fangtooths), Anomalopidae (flashlight or lanterneye fish), Monocentridae (pineapple and pinecone fish), Trachichthyidae (roughies, sawbellies, and slimeheads), Holocentridae (squirrelfish and soldierfish)

**Subfamilies** Holocentridae: Holocentrinae (squirrelfish), Myripristinae (soldierfish)

**Order** Beryciformes

**Number of species** Anoplogastridae: 2 in 1 genus; Anomalopidae: 8 in 6 genera; Monocentridae: 4 in 2 genera; Trachichthyidae: around 44 in 8 genera; Holocentridae: around 83 in 8 genera

**Size** From 2 in (5 cm) to 30 in (75 cm)

**Key features** Longish to oval body shape; body scales range from very small to large and platelike; head from blunt to more pointed, moderately large to very large; light organ under eye or on lower jaw; eyes relatively large to large in most species (small in fangtooths); powerful fanglike teeth (fangtooths); one dorsal fin (spines in front, soft rays in back); pronounced dorsal fin notch (lanternfish) or two separate fins (pineapple fish); variable coloration: yellow through red to brown and black; some species have light or dark patterns, luminescence produced inside bodies

**Breeding** Few details available; eggs and sperm released into water where fertilization takes place; no parental care; eggs take a few weeks to hatch; larvae usually live among plankton for some time

**Diet** Mainly fish; some invertebrates

**Habitat** Relatively shallow tropical and subtropical, also temperate, waters; deepwater species (fangtooth) down to 16,400 ft (5,000 m); many in caves or under ledges during day, rise to surface at night.

**Distribution** Atlantic, Indian, and Pacific Oceans

⤒ *The 6-inch (15-cm) common fangtooth (*Anoplogaster cornuta*) occurs between 1,640 and 16,400 feet (500–5,000 m). These predators are, in turn, hunted by tuna and marlin.*

# Fangtooths and Relatives

Anoplogastridae, Anomalopidae
Monocentridae, Trachichthyidae, Holocentridae

*The fangtooth is a fearsome predator. It has a huge mouth in relation to its size and sharp fangs to match. There is no escape for any fish that is seized by this brown-bodied hunter.*

THE MAJOR FAMILIES IN THE ORDER Beryciformes have some 141 species in 25 genera—from the fearsome fangtooths, flashlight fish, pineapple fish, and roughies (families Anoplogastridae, Anomalopidae, Monocentridae, and Trachichthyidae, respectively) to the family Holocentridae, with its subfamilies of squirrelfish (Holocentrinae) and soldierfish (Myripristinae).

## Dramatic Fangtooth Changes

The common fangtooth (*Anoplogaster cornuta*) lives in deep water from 1,640 feet (500 m) down to 16,400 feet (5,000 m) and is one of two species in the family Anoplogastridae. The other is the smaller shorthorn fangtooth (*A. brachycera*), just over 2.4 inches (6 cm) long; also a predator, it is found in shallower waters from 3,300 to 4,920 feet (1,000–1,500 m) in the western Pacific and Atlantic Oceans.

The young of these fish look very different from the adults, with a spine on top of the head and another on the bottom edge of one of the gill-cover bones. They can grow so large and last for such a long time (until half adult size) that for about 100 years the young and adult fangtooth forms were believed to belong to separate species. The juveniles' true identity was not realized until 1955 as "intermediate" specimens began to be collected.

## Flashlights and Lanterns

The remarkable flashlight or lanterneye fish belong to a small family (Anomalopidae) of six genera and eight species. Mainly tropical Indo-Pacific fish, they have a patchy distribution.

*⊕ This large-eyed common fangtooth (Anoplogaster cornuta), seen here in California waters, has a hard, bony body unlike most deep-sea fish. Very few prey items escape the sharp teeth of this fearsome predator, even though it is only 6 inches (15 cm) long.*

Most species are small, but the splitfin flashlight fish (*Anomalops katoptron*) grows much larger than the rest, up to 13.8 inches (35 cm). The smallest species, probably the least known member in the group—*Parmops coruscans* from the Society islands in Tahiti— is just over 2 inches (5 cm) long.

Flashlight fish are easily distinguished from all other light-producing fish because their light organ consists of a pouch under each eye and is opened and closed by a skin fold. This light,

which can be switched on and off, serves several purposes. For example, it helps members of the shoal keep in touch with each other; also, the eerie light attracts zooplankton, its main food source. In addition, switching the light organ off and changing position in midwater helps confuse predators.

Despite having light organs, flashlight fish are not deepwater specialists. In fact, some species spend their lives in shallow water—the Gulf flashlight fish (*Phthanophaneron harveyi*)

⊙ *Prickly fins and a yellow body give the pineapple fish* (Monocentris japonica) *its characteristic name.*

from the Gulf of California rarely, if ever, ventures deeper than 120 feet (36 m), while the eyelight fish (*Photoblepharon palpebratum*) tends to stay above 82 feet (25 m). However, they do spend much of the day in caves or other shelters, coming out at night to feed. Their deeper-water relatives do likewise (often in shoals), rising toward the surface to feed.

## Pineapples and Pinecones

Closely related to the flashlight fish, but looking quite different, are the pineapple, pinecone, coat-of-mail, or knight fish of the family Monocentridae. The family has only four species and they are distributed in the tropical and sub-tropical regions of the Indo-Pacific.

The body is stumpy, almost oval, and is covered in large, heavily built, platelike scales.

## Bacterial Flashlights

The eight flashlight fish are among the 1,000 to 1,500 fish species in nearly 190 genera that are capable of producing light. They can be divided into two groups:
• Fish that have special organs (photophores) that generate light through a chain of chemical reactions
• Fish that use the light produced by "symbiotic" bacteria (dissimilar organisms that mutually benefit one another)

Flashlight fish belong to the second group. They keep colonies of "luminescent" (light-producing) bacteria in specially adapted cheek pouches, living in symbiosis, or harmony, with them. The fish provide the nourishment that the bacteria require, and in return, the bacteria help the fish by producing light. Thus both parties gain from what is a most unusual partnership.

Flashlight fish cannot control either the intensity or the duration of the light that the bacteria generate. However, having these lights permanently "switched on" would be a great disadvantage to the fish, especially since it would make them highly visible to predators. Over time flashlight fish have evolved a cheek flap, or "lid," that they can extend over the bacteria-containing organ, thus effectively "switching off" their lights by hiding them from view.

With their prickly dorsal and pelvic fins and yellowish body color, it is easy to see how one of the common names—pineapple fish—may have arisen. In addition to being stout, the pelvic fin spine can also be locked in a raised position. Thus pineapple and pinecone fish have efficient defenses, hence the reference in one of their names—coat-of-mail fish.

While looking quite different from the flashlight fish, these four family members have, like their relatives, light organs packed with symbiotic, luminescent bacteria. Unlike the flashlight fish, though, pineapple and pinecone fish cannot "switch" their organs on and off. Instead, the light emitted by the bacteria looks different according to the amount of natural light that is available. During the day the bacterial light appears orange and is less obvious than it is in its characteristic, bright blue-green night colors.

The four species in this family can be split into two groups, easily distinguished by the position and size of their light organs. In the pineapple fish, knight fish, or luminescent pinecone fish—also called the port and starboard bightfish or lightfish (*Cleidopus gloriamaris*) from Australia's western and southern coasts—the light organ is large and is located along the side of each lower jaw. At 8.7 inches (22 cm) it is the largest family member.

## Spiny Cheeks

**A**lthough the names squirrelfish and soldierfish are frequently used loosely to refer to fish belonging to the family Holocentridae, there are differences between them. Of them the most easily observed one (although there are others) is the presence of a strong spine on the cheek in squirrelfish and its absence in the soldierfish, except in one species—the spinycheek soldierfish (*Corniger spinosus*).

Therefore the squirrelfish are placed in a subfamily—the Holocentrinae (genera *Holocentrus*, *Neoniphon*, and *Sargocentron*), while the soldierfish form the subfamily Myripristinae (genera *Corniger*, *Myripristis*, *Ostichthys*, *Plectrypops*, and *Pristilepis*).

In the other three species belonging to the genus *Monocentris* the light organ is smaller, positioned near the tip of the lower jaw. These species are also smaller, the smallest being one of the pinecone fish (*M. reedi*); there are also two species from the southeastern Pacific that grow to nearly 4 inches (10 cm).

Like the flashlight fish, the pineapple and pinecone fish use the light generated by their bacteria both for communication with other members of the shoal and to attract their main food items (zooplankton and shrimp) at night.

### Slime-headed, Saw-bellied Roughies

The roughies, slimeheads, or sawbellies form a family (Trachichthyidae) of around 44 species.

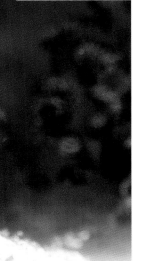

⊕ *A big-eyed, striped redcoat squirrelfish* (Sargocentron rubrum) *is in stark contrast to the deep green vegetation in the Andaman Sea off Thailand. Squirrelfish range in size from a dwarf species at just 3.2 inches (8 cm) up to 24 inches (60 cm) in length.*

⊖ *A millet butterflyfish* (Chaetodon miliaris) *with blotcheye soldierfish* (Myripristis berndti) *on a sea reef.*

They are characterized by skin-covered ridges of bone on the head, with mucus-rich areas in between—hence the slimehead "label." The sawbelly and roughy nametags come from the row of large hard plates (scutes) along the belly.

Roughies are predatory fish with elongated, oval-shaped bodies and large mouths. They feed on fish and a wide range of invertebrates, including squid, shrimp, and other crustaceans. Some species—like those belonging to the genera *Aulotrachichthys*, *Paratrachichthys*, and *Sorosichthys*—are luminescent; but unlike the flashlight fish and pineapple fish, roughies generate their light within their bodies.

Many roughies are fished commercially, especially the orange roughy (*Hoplostethus atlanticus*), which is probably the largest species at around 30 inches (75 cm) long and weighing 15.4 pounds (7 kg). Reportedly living to 149 years, it is also one of the longest-living species of fish known. In addition, it is probably the deepest diving roughy, having been recorded at a depth of 5,935 feet (1,809 m).

### Squirrelfish and Soldierfish

The largest family (Holocentridae) in the order Beryciformes is that formed by the squirrelfish and soldierfish. With around 83 species in eight genera, some are fished commercially, although not on a large scale. Some species, like the

redcoat (*Sargocentron rubrum*), have a venomous spine on the cheek, but they are, nevertheless, good food fish.

Between 1945 and the early 1970s the redcoat was introduced from the Red Sea into some eastern Mediterranean locations where it has become established. Some other species, like the common squirrelfish (*Holocentrus adscensionis*), are known to cause ciguatera poisoning, a severe type of digestive poisoning that can result in death—but this only occurs when contaminated specimens are eaten.

Many species spend much of the day hiding in crevices, caves, and under ledges. At such times they tend to adopt "cryptic coloration," which helps them blend in with their shady surroundings, thus protecting them from predators. However, as darkness falls, they become active, change into bolder colors, and venture out to feed.

Although squirrelfish and soldierfish have large eyes, they are not deepwater fish, with most species found at depths of less than 655 feet (200 m); quite a few are mostly confined to shallow or very shallow habitats. However, since they are most active at night, their large eyes allow them to navigate around the reef and to find food (mainly crustaceans and small fish) in the same sort of dark conditions that deepwater fish live in day or night.

### Two Other Families

There are two additional families in the order Beryciformes—the Diretmidae (spinyfins) and the Berycidae (alfonsinos and redfish).

The four spinyfins are deepwater species, found at depths around 6,560 feet (2,000 m), and grow to a maximum size of about 14.6 inches (37 cm).

The nine large-eyed, large-mouthed redfish and alfonsinos range from depths of between 655 and 1,970 feet (200–600 m). Slightly larger than the spinyfins, they can attain a maximum size of around 24 inches (60 cm).

John Dory (*Zeus faber*)

**Common name** Dories and relatives

**Families** Zeidae (dories), Oreosomatidae (oreos), Caproidae (boarfish)

**Subfamilies** Caproidae: Some classifications divide this famly into Antigoniinae and Caproinae

**Order** Zeiformes

**Number of species** Zeidae: 14 in 7 genera; Oreosomatidae: 10 in 4 genera; Caproidae: 12 in 2 genera

**Size** From around 2.5 in (6.3 cm) to about 36 in (90 cm)

**Key features** Body highly compressed in all species, very deep in some species; snout pointed to varying degrees; mouth from quite small to extremely large, extendable in all species; large eyes; dorsal fin has spiny front half, soft-rayed back; small strong spines run along both sides of dorsal and anal fins (dories), front dorsal spines very long (John Dory and others); scales generally small, with sandpaper effect (oreos, boarfish); variable coloration: mottled, silvery-gray to dark, also reds

**Breeding** Eggs and sperm released into water where they are fertilized; in some species eggs are fertilized inside female, then released; no parental care of either eggs or larvae

**Diet** Fish and invertebrates; also salps (sea squirts)

**Habitat** Most occur close to seafloor over muddy, sandy, or rocky bottoms, also reefs; a few enter brackish water; all recognized as marine fish; depth from very shallow water, e.g., 16 ft (5 m), to nearly 5,100 ft (1,550 m)

**Distribution** Antarctic, Atlantic, Indian, and Pacific Oceans, some into major seas like Mediterranean

↑ *The John Dory (*Zeus faber*) is also known as St. Peter's fish. Together with the Cape Dory (*Zeus capensis*) they are the longest of the dories, each growing to a maximum of 36 inches (90 cm).*

# Dories and Relatives
Zeidae, Oreosomatidae, Caproidae

*Dories are all superb stealth hunters. They can drift undetected up to their prey and then strike with deadly accuracy, sucking in their victim with their huge "hinged" tube mouth.*

THERE ARE 36 SPECIES IN THE 13 GENERA within the three main families of the order Zeiformes—the dories (family Zeidae), the oreos (family Oreosomatidae), and the boarfish (family Caproidae). There are also three smaller families in the order Zeiformes (see box).

### John, Peter, and Friends

The John Dory (*Zeus faber*), in particular, is an excellently camouflaged species that has hugely elongated rays in the dorsal fin. It tends to keep close to the bottom, swimming in a gentle, almost drifting manner that makes it look like a clump of seaweed. It is also ultrathin, which makes it very difficult to spot head-on. Both these characteristics help make it a supreme predator; it feeds on herrings, anchovies, and other shoaling fish, as well as on crustaceans, squid, and octopus. Large John Dories can grow to nearly 36 inches (90 cm) long and weigh about 17.6 pounds (8 kg)—a relatively light weight in relation to the body size.

Along with several of its closest relatives the John Dory is considered an excellent food fish and is popular over much of its range (but, oddly, not in Africa). It extends over much of the temperate and subtropical world, occurring in very shallow water, from 16 feet (5 m) down to relatively deep water, at 1,310 feet (400 m), and, occasionally, in brackish water.

The John Dory has 13 close relatives in the family Zeidae. Several species are less well known, and not all carry the prominent black spots on the body that the John Dory does but are silvery-bodied. The silver Dory (*Cyttus australis*), a 16-inch (40-cm) Australian species

⊕ *The John Dory (Zeus faber) has a worldwide distribution. The fish is easily identified by its characteristic large dark spot (found on both sides of its body), which is surrounded by a lighter-colored ring.*

that, like many of its fellow family members, is fished commercially, is aptly named and has no body spots. In contrast, the silvery John Dory (*Zenopsis conchifer*) is silvery-gray but has the two prominent spots. It is widely distributed in the western Indian Ocean and both sides of the Atlantic; with a length of between 30 and 32 inches (76–81 cm) and weighing up to 7 pounds (3.2 kg), it is another important food-fish member of the family.

This relatively large-size, low-weight ratio is typical of dories because of their highly compressed bodies, but they are considered

excellent eating because they produce large, delicately textured fillets with few bones.

The breeding habits of dories is not well known. In most species eggs and sperm are released into the water where fertilization takes place. However, in the mirror Dory (*Zenopsis nebulosus*) the eggs are fertilized while still inside the female and then released. The larvae spend some time among plankton, gradually changing into the typical shape for their species. In the John Dory juveniles can take as long as four years to mature and then can live for another eight years.

↑ *This larval boarfish (Antigonia species) is mesopelagic, occurring at depths from 984 to 1,640 feet (300–500 m) on the upper continental shelf of the Atlantic Ocean.*

## Deep-diving Oreos

Looking like large-eyed, short-finned versions of dories, the oreos (family Oreosomatidae) are a small family of dorylike species, found in the Antarctic, Atlantic, Indian, and Pacific Oceans, despite having just ten or so members.

Their sizes range from a little over 6 inches (15 cm) long in *Neocyttus acanthorhynchus* from the Indian Ocean to just over 24 inches (60 cm) in the smooth oreo (*Pseudocyttus maculatus*), a commercially fished species from the South Pacific and both coasts of the South Atlantic Oceans.

Like dories, several oreos are good food fish, including the black oreo (*Allocyttus niger*) from the southwest Pacific, found at depths between 1,840 and 4,265 feet (560–1,300 m), though it is not the deepest species. The two most outstanding species in this respect are the smooth oreo, with a depth range down to 4,920 feet (1,500 m), and the ox-eyed oreo (*Oreosoma atlanticum*), an especially large-eyed fish found down to nearly 5,100 feet (1,550 m).

Despite being mostly deepwater species, oreos produce floating eggs and planktonic larvae, just like dories. In addition, several oreo

## Extendable Mouths

A dory's mouth is amazing. When it is shot out (faster than the eye can see), it forms a huge "hinged" tube that can suck in any prey within range. While none of the species are high-speed swimmers, they are all superb stealth hunters that can drift undetected up to their prey, such as fish and invertebrates, and then strike with deadly accuracy.

# Golden-edged St. Peter's Fish

The origins of the name "John Dory" are uncertain, especially since there is no record of it having been named in honor of anyone called John Dory. One of the (perhaps) more plausible explanations is that it is derived from the French *jaune d'orée*, which can be translated as "with yellow border or edge." Presumably, this could refer to the yellowish-golden tinge that John Dories have on their bodies, as well as on the edges of their fins.

In many countries this species is also known as the St. Peter's fish. The origins of this particular label are even more obscure. It relates to the two black spots on the center of the John Dory's body—one on each side—which are said to represent St. Peter's thumb and forefinger print.

species, like the smooth oreo and black oreo, are known to fertilize their eggs internally.

## The Red-colored Boarfish

The boarfish (like oreos) look like dories without their elongated dorsal fin rays. The deepbody boarfish (*Antigonia capros*), however, looks like a dory that has run into a rockface and been squeezed from nose to tail.

The 12 species that make up this family (Caproidae) have reddish bodies (unlike the oreos or the dories) and a feature that they share with the oreos—small scales with a sandpaper feel. The snout is pointed (but least so in the deepbody boarfish), and the mouth is considerably smaller (in relation to the head and body) than in the dories. Nevertheless, it can still be extended a long way. Most of the species also have large eyes, as the oreos do.

Although two boarfish—the deepbody boarfish and the common boarfish (*Capros aper*)—grow to around 12 inches (30 cm) long, neither is considered an important food fish. Sometimes the common boarfish is caught (because of its shoaling habits) in large numbers in trawl nets; if that happens, the catch is

# The Other Dories

### Family Macrurocyttidae

This family consists of five species in two genera. They are considerably longer-bodied than their relatives and are generally poorly known. *Macrurocyttus acanthopodus* has been collected at 2,880 feet (878 m), but we do not know if it extends above or below this depth. "*Acantho*" means "spiny," and "*podus*" refers to limbs, feet, or (in this case) fins. Applying these meanings to *M. acanthopodus*, we find it has long spines both on the dorsal and the pelvic fins. It also has very large eyes, indicating that it lives in deep water.

### Family Parazenidae

The parazen (*Parazen pacificus*) is the sole representative of its family. It is a western central Atlantic species that is reported to grow between 5.5 and 10 inches (14–25 cm) in length. It is elongated with a large eye and large, pointed mouth that is highly extendable. Unusually, it has two lateral lines running from behind the gills toward the caudal peduncle, but joining up before reaching there.

### Family Grammicolepididae

The tinselfish, as this family is known, contains just two species. The smaller one—the spotted tinselfish (*Xenolepidichthys dalgleishi*)—measures 6 inches (15 cm) and has a wide distribution in deep water on both sides of the Atlantic, the western Pacific, and the Indian Oceans. It is a deep-bodied species with large eyes and the characteristic extendable mouth. The much larger thorny tinselfish (*Grammicolepis branchiusculus*) grows to around 25 inches (64 cm) and has a longer body (in relation to its height). It, too, can be found at great depths—down to 2,625 feet (800 m). Also, the scales of the tinselfish are unusual in that they are taller than they are long.

⟵ *The common boarfish* (Capros aper) *occurs in the Atlantic and Mediterranean waters. Together with the deepbody boarfish* (Antigonia capros) *they are the largest of the species, with a length of 12 inches (30 cm).*

usually processed into fishmeal. The deepbody boarfish is also fished commercially, but on quite a minor scale.

The largest members of their family are the common boarfish and deepbody boarfish. The smallest representative is *Antigonia indica*, which is found in the Indian Ocean—as its name indicates. It is more orange-colored than its relatives and only grows to about 2.5 inches (6.3 cm) in length.

# Sticklebacks, Sea Horses, and Relatives

Order Gasterosteiformes

Sticklebacks and sea horses look very different not only from each other, but to tubesnouts, seamoths, razorfish, trumpetfish, and cornetfish as well. Yet they are more closely related to each other than it seems at first. With a total of some 316 other species they form the order Gasterosteiformes (gasteriform fish).

## Scutes and Pelvics Hold the Key

Their most obvious shared characteristic is that their bodies are covered by bony plates (scutes), not by scales; but there are exceptions. For example, some populations of three-spined stickleback (*Gasterosteus aculeatus*) have no scales at all, yet they are undeniably sticklebacks. So too, is the scuteless Greek nine-spined stickleback (*Pungitius hellenicus*), also in the family Gasterosteidae.

Similarly, a combination of tubelike snouts, scutes, or isolated dorsal spines shows that tubesnouts (family Aulorhynchidae), seamoths (family Pegasidae), and ghost pipefish (family Solenostomidae) are relatives of sea horses (family Syngnathidae) and sticklebacks.

The Korean sand eel (*Hypoptychus dybowskii*) is the sole representative of its family (Hypoptychidae) but has no scutes, scales, or dorsal fin spines. However, the lack of a pelvic girdle and pelvic fins makes this fish a member of the same order as some sticklebacks, sea horses, and pipefish. This characteristic, along with skeletal features and biology, makes the association clearer.

Scientists' classifications differ on how closely related some species, genera, or families are. In this set Nelson (1994) is used but with recent updates. Accordingly, the order is divided into 10 families (see panel below).

### Order Gasterosteiformes: 10 families, about 316 species, including:

**Family** Syngnathidae—52 genera and about 270 species (sea horses, pipefish, pipehorses, and seadragons)

**Family** Centriscidae—5 genera and 13 species (snipefish and shrimpfish)

**Family** Gasterosteidae—5 genera and 11 species (sticklebacks)

## Trumpets, Cornets, Snipes, and Shrimps

The trumpetfish (family Aulostomidae) and the cornetfish (family Fistularidae) form two closely related families. With their extended snouts they resemble sea horses, pipefish, and close relatives, though not sticklebacks.

Trumpetfish have isolated spines in front of the dorsal fin, just like sticklebacks, but lack body scutes. However, cornetfish lack the dorsal spines but have a small scute.

The snipefish and shrimpfish (considered as separate families in some classifications) are here included in a single family (Centriscidae) to which bellowfish and razorfish also belong. All of them lack the isolated dorsal fin spines, but they do have body scutes and snouts.

While they are the most easily observed features that suggest some kind of relationship between the above three families and the sticklebacks, sea horses, and their kin, there are other internal factors that are much more difficult to detect and assess. Nevertheless, when put together, they are all thought to show that all three are "legitimate" family members of the stickleback order.

## Paradoxical Fish

As its name suggests, *Indostomus paradoxus* is a paradoxical fish, with scutes, isolated dorsal spines, and a tubelike snout, which seem to indicate that it should belong with the same suborder as all the above fish.

However, so little is known about this fish that ever since its discovery in 1926, scientists have differed with regard to its relationship (or lack of one) to other members of the order—especially when there are already differences of opinion as to the internal relationship between the various families. The point is discussed further for this small family (Indostomidae) of armored sticklebacks in the sea horses, pipefish, and allies section.

⊖ *A pygmy sea horse* (Hippocampus bargibanti) *wraps its prehensile tail around a strand of gorgonian coral in waters off Sulawesi, Indonesia. It belongs to the Hippocampinae, a subfamily of the family Syngnathidae.*

 **SEE ALSO** Eel, Korean Sand **39**:28; Sticklebacks **39**:30; Seamoths **39**:36; Sea Horses **39**:38; Trumpetfish and Cornetfish **39**:48

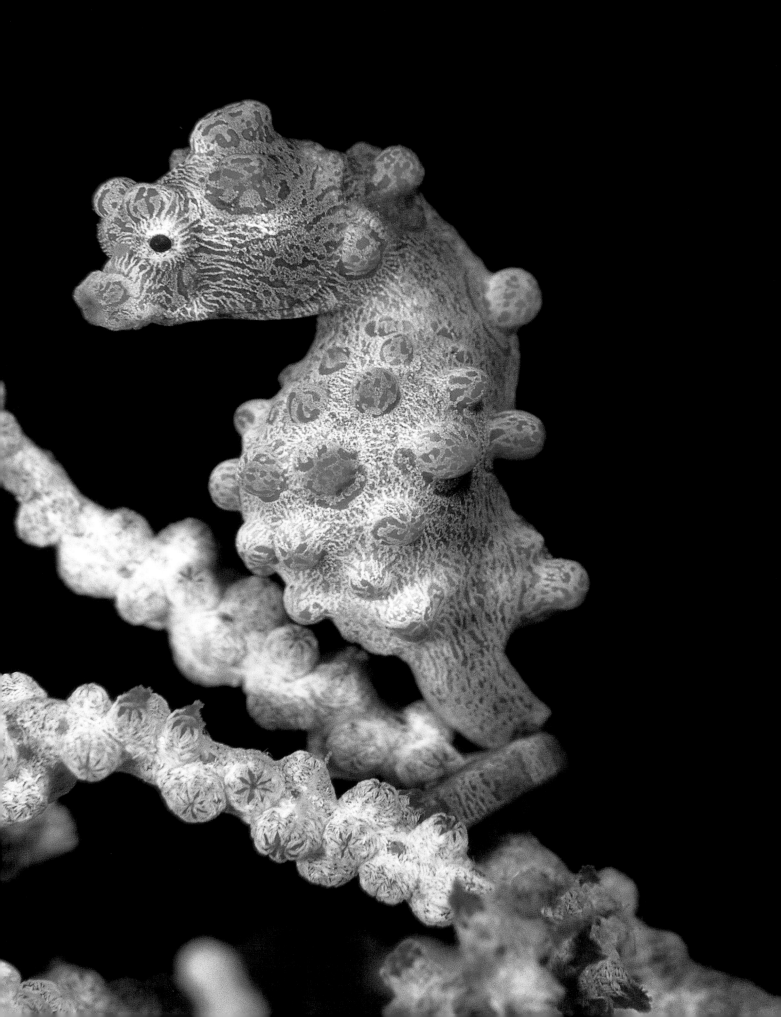

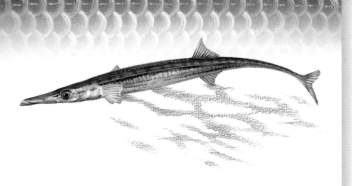

# Korean Sand Eel and Tubesnouts

Hypoptychidae, Aulorhynchidae

*When is an eel not an eel? When it is a sand eel. It takes a great deal of imagination to find eel-like characteristics in this fish. However, superficially it does look like the "true" sand eels or sand lances.*

THE KOREAN SAND EEL (*HYPOPTYCHUS dybowskii*) is a small, 3.4-inch (8.5-cm), elongated fish that lives in shoals near the bottom, in shallow water down to 66 feet (20 m). It is a very prolific fish; it has to be because scientists believe its lifespan is just over one year. In fact, it is estimated that a population can double itself in as little as 15 months.

This scaleless fish (an eel-like characteristic) has its dorsal and anal fins set well back on the body, quite close to the slightly forked tail; there are no pelvic fins, but pectorals are well formed. Spawning occurs in June/July in very shallow water, often between high and low tides, with the eggs deposited on seaweed. The Korean sand eel is found in the North Pacific, between Sakhalin in Russia and northern Japan. It occurs in large numbers and is fished commercially.

## Sand Eels Compared

The Korean sand eel's closest relatives are not other "eels" but the tubemouths (family Aulorhynchidae) and the sticklebacks (family Gasterosteidae). The "true" sand eels (mentioned above) are not true eels either. They belong to the family Ammodytidae, also known as sand lances. They are perchlike fish (order Perciformes), much more closely related to stargazers (family Uranoscopidae), weeverfish (family Trachinidae), and blennies (family Blenniidae) than to true eels, from which they differ considerably.

Korean sand eels are different from the sand eels or sand lances by having short-based dorsal anal fins, a much larger eye, and equal-

---

**Tubesnout (*Aulorhynchus flavidus*)**

**Common name** Korean sand eel and tubesnouts

**Families** Hypoptychidae (sand eel), Aulorhynchidae (tubesnouts)

**Order** Gasterosteiformes

**Number of species** 1 in 1 genus (sand eel); 2 in 2 monotypic genera (tubesnout, tubenose)

**Size** From around 3.4 in (8.5 cm) to 7.1 in (18 cm)

**Key features** Slim, elongated bodies: scaleless (sand eel), bony plates, or scutes (tubesnouts); pointed snouts (particularly tubenose, tubesnout); eyes relatively large (sand eel), smaller (tubesnout); dorsal and anal fins set well back on body but preceded by up to 26 spines (tubesnout); tail forked; pelvic fin absent in sand eel; coloration: drab, darker above, fading to lighter along belly (sand eel); brownish above, fading to creamy white below, with longitudinal brown band on body (tubesnouts); male tubesnouts turn red during the breeding season

**Breeding** Eggs laid: in June/July among seaweed in very shallow water (sand eel); in gill chamber of sea squirts (tubesnose); in nest built by male among seaweed (tubesnout); male guards eggs until they hatch 2–3 weeks later and protects larvae for short time

**Diet** Small invertebrates; also fish larvae

**Habitat** Shallow sandy areas (sand eel) rarely below 66 ft (20 m); shallow water with sandy, rocky, or heavily vegetated bottoms, frequently found in shoals near surface (tubesnout)

**Distribution** North Pacific from Japan and Korea to Sea of Okhotsk, east of Russia (sand eel), eastern Pacific (tubesnout), and northwest Pacific (tubenose)

*⬆ The 7.1-inch (18-cm) tubesnout (*Aulorhynchus flavidus*) is found over sandy or rocky bottoms, eelgrass, or kelp beds in the eastern Pacific. In the breeding season the long snout of the male turns a bright red.*

**SEE ALSO** Eels and Eel-like Fish **33**:62; Blennies **40**:90

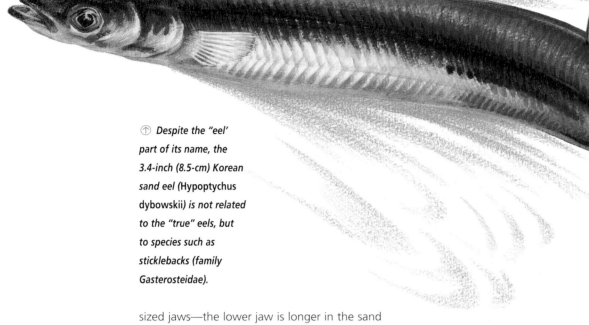

⊙ *Despite the "eel' part of its name, the 3.4-inch (8.5-cm) Korean sand eel (*Hypoptychus dybowskii*) is not related to the "true" eels, but to species such as sticklebacks (family Gasterosteidae).*

sized jaws—the lower jaw is longer in the sand eels or sand lances. The latter are also larger: up to 12 inches (30 cm), compared with the 3.4-inch (8.5-cm) Korean sand eel.

### Stretched-out "Sticklebacks"
The tubesnouts (family Aulorhynchidae) look a little like stretched-out sticklebacks—more specifically, like an even slimmer version of the ultraslim fifteen-spine stickleback (*Spinachia spinachia*). The similarities are such that some scientists believe one of the tubesnouts—the tubenose (*Aulichthys japonicus*)—should be grouped with the sticklebacks. Others have a different opinion, believing that this tubenose's nearest relative is the Korean sand eel. The debate continues, with each point of view being vigorously defended. Yet there are only two species within the family—the tubenose and the tubesnout (*Aulorhynchus flavidus*). At least, such is the case at the moment, until more is discovered about the relationship between the two species—and also between them and their relatives.

Both have elongated bodies with bony plates down the sides—a feature that they share with most sticklebacks. There are also up to 26 short isolated spines along the back, followed by a soft dorsal fin (again, another stickleback characteristic). In the tubesnout males have further stickleback characteristics in that they develop red coloration during the breeding season. Also in the tubesnout this coloration appears on its snout; but for the three-spine stickleback (*Gasterosteus aculeatus*) its chest reddens during the breeding season.

Male tubesnouts also build nests among seaweed—and defend them, just as the sticklebacks do. In sharp contrast, the tubenose lays its eggs inside the gill chamber of sea squirts (class Ascidiacea), then abandons them. The tubesnout (an eastern Pacific species) tends to spawn during midspring, while the tubenose (a northwest Pacific species) spawns a little later, usually during early summer. Once the eggs hatch, the larvae spend some time among plankton, feeding on tiny organisms; as they develop, they graduate to slightly larger foods that include fish larvae, small crustaceans, and other invertebrates.

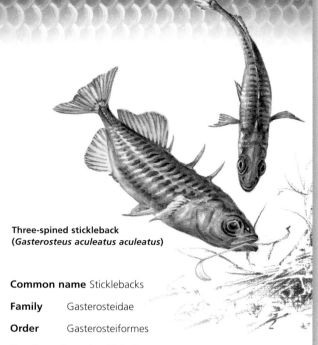

**Three-spined stickleback**
(*Gasterosteus aculeatus aculeatus*)

**Common name** Sticklebacks

**Family** Gasterosteidae

**Order** Gasterosteiformes

**Number of species** 11 in 5 genera

**Size** From 2 in (5 cm) to 9 in (23 cm)

**Key features** Elongated, compressed body, with bony plates (scutes) running lengthwise; pointed head; mouth angled upward; eyes relatively large; row of isolated spines running along back and in front of soft dorsal fin; number of spines varies within species, but no spines in Greek nine-spine stickleback; sometimes pelvic spine and fin lacking; caudal peduncle slim to very slim; coloration: variable, especially in males; blue, green, brown, black, and red (particularly intense during breeding)

**Breeding** Female lays eggs in nest built by male; young hatch 7–10 days later, protected by male

**Diet** Invertebrates; also fish eggs, larvae, and small fish

**Habitat** Pure fresh water through brackish water to fully marine; vegetated areas (preferably with no movement or light currents) and fine-grained bottoms; mostly found in very shallow water, but some occur down to 180 ft (55 m)

**Distribution** Widely distributed in Northern Hemisphere

**Status** World Conservation Union lists Greek nine-spine stickleback (*Pungitius hellenicus*) as Critically Endangered

*⬆ This 4.3-inch (11-cm) male three-spined stickleback (*Gasterosteus aculeatus aculeatus*) constructs a nest from plant material in which the female will lay her eggs. A male's chest turns bright red or orange in the breeding season.*

# Sticklebacks

Gasterosteidae

*In the Northern Hemisphere the stickleback can easily be observed in ponds, ditches, or streams. These small, brilliantly colored prickly fish are usually the three-spined sticklebacks.*

DESPITE ITS WORLDWIDE FAME, THE THREE-SPINED stickleback (*Gasterosteus aculeatus aculeatus*) is the topic of much debate. Along with other aspects of its lifestyle its feeding and breeding habits have been studied in great detail for many years and are quite well known.

## Adaptable Stickleback

The three-spined stickleback has a very wide geographic distribution. In North America it occurs from Baffin Island and western Hudson Bay southward to Chesapeake Bay in Virginia, but not in many central areas except for Lake Ontario. On the Pacific coast it is found from Alaska down to Baja California in Mexico. It is also occurs in Greenland, Iceland, and the Pacific coast of Asia. In Europe it is found in most rivers, except large sections of the Danube River. It also extends into the Mediterranean and Black Seas and North Africa, from Algeria to Iran in the Middle East.

This fish is extremely versatile and is found in a range of habitats from fresh and brackish water to fully marine conditions—in pure freshwater shallow streams and ditches to estuaries and shallow coastal waters to a depth of nearly 90 feet (27 m). Such fish, which are capable of living in both fresh and sea waters, are described as anadromous species.

In view of this stickleback's extensive range and adaptability to diverse environmental conditions there are widely differing opinions on the species as a whole, as well as the nature of some of its isolated populations.

## How Many Three-spines?

One main question, to which no satisfactory answer has been found, is how many species or

*⬇ The spines on this adult ten-spined stickleback (*Pungitius pungitius pungitius*) are clearly well developed. The ten-spine is one of two subspecies of the nine-spined stickleback (*P. pungitius*).*

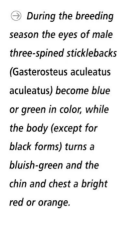

⊙ *During the breeding season the eyes of male three-spined sticklebacks (Gasterosteus aculeatus aculeatus) become blue or green in color, while the body (except for black forms) turns a bluish-green and the chin and chest a bright red or orange.*

subspecies of the three-spined sticklebacks exist. The answer is very complex.

When a species is as widely distributed as the three-spined stickleback, it is subjected to different environmental influences, such as type and abundance of food supply, temperature, quality, speed, depth, and clarity of water, amount and type of vegetation, even types of predator—they can all differ. Also, isolated populations cannot interbreed.

## Separated Populations

Such factors all have an effect on resident fish that subsequently can evolve along different paths, so they begin to look and behave quite differently from one another. If these changes persist for long enough, or result in very different characteristics, there will come a time when separated populations will not be able to interbreed even if reunited by a natural event (like two rivers joining up) or for experimental studies. Thus, over time, a fish that was one species when it began spreading evolves into two or more distinct species or subspecies.

This has happened to the three-spined stickleback to such an extent that scientists are not sure how many three-spines now exist. For

example, freshwater populations are generally spotted, with some brown and greenish tones along the back that fade to silvery on the belly. However, types that migrate between salt water and fresh water tend to lack brown tones and are more bluish-black. This darkening is taken further, in some isolated populations, in which males do not develop the same red throat and chest, green or blue eyes, or brilliant blue-green body sheen of their close relatives. The length is also different between freshwater and marine forms, with the latter growing larger—to 4.3 inches (11 cm) rather than 3.2 inches (8 cm).

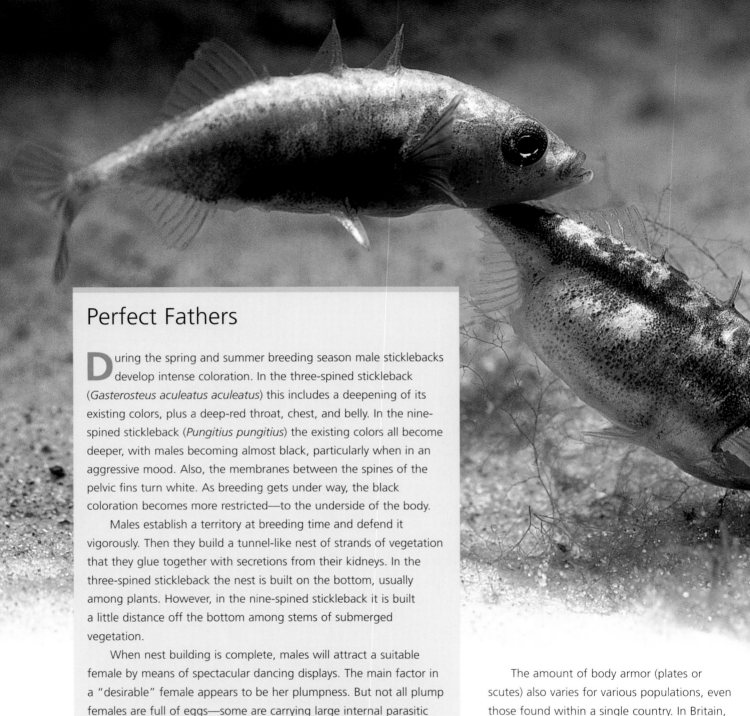

# Perfect Fathers

**D**uring the spring and summer breeding season male sticklebacks develop intense coloration. In the three-spined stickleback (*Gasterosteus aculeatus aculeatus*) this includes a deepening of its existing colors, plus a deep-red throat, chest, and belly. In the nine-spined stickleback (*Pungitius pungitius*) the existing colors all become deeper, with males becoming almost black, particularly when in an aggressive mood. Also, the membranes between the spines of the pelvic fins turn white. As breeding gets under way, the black coloration becomes more restricted—to the underside of the body.

Males establish a territory at breeding time and defend it vigorously. Then they build a tunnel-like nest of strands of vegetation that they glue together with secretions from their kidneys. In the three-spined stickleback the nest is built on the bottom, usually among plants. However, in the nine-spined stickleback it is built a little distance off the bottom among stems of submerged vegetation.

When nest building is complete, males will attract a suitable female by means of spectacular dancing displays. The main factor in a "desirable" female appears to be her plumpness. But not all plump females are full of eggs—some are carrying large internal parasitic tapeworms that make their bellies swell. Assuming the female is able to breed, she will enter the nest and lay up to 600 eggs, leaving the male to fertilize them. Then he will attempt to attract further females until, in the three-spined stickleback, up to 1,000 eggs have been laid and fertilized.

The male stands guard over the eggs until the first hatchlings occur, about 7 to 10 days after laying. The newborns remain close to the nest for a week, protected by their father, before they disperse.

The amount of body armor (plates or scutes) also varies for various populations, even those found within a single country. In Britain, for example, three distinct forms are known. The "trachura" form has scutes running the whole length of the body—from head to caudal peduncle. The "semiarmata" form has incomplete and variable body armor, while the "leiurus" type has no scutes at all. Therefore, do these forms belong to the same species or subspecies—or are they separate species?

Currently the above forms are considered to be members of a single, highly variable

⊕ *The pointed head, large eyes, and upward angled mouth are clearly visible as this fifteen-spined stickleback (Spinachia spinachia) peeps out from seaweed in Cork County, Ireland. Its alternative name is the sea stickleback.*

⊖ *This pair of three-spined sticklebacks (Gasterosteus aculeatus aculeatus) are about to enter their nest that the male has built on the bottom among plants. Note the male's red breeding color along the underside of his body.*

subspecies of the three-spined stickleback—*Gasterosteus aculeatus aculeatus*. Three other subspecies are also recognized. One from Japan, where it is restricted to small freshwater streams, has a slightly smaller head but no common name (*G. a. microcephalus*). The Santa Ana stickleback (*G. a. santaeannae*) is a North American fish found in fresh, brackish, and marine waters. The unarmored three-spined stickleback (*G. a. williamsoni*) from southern California lacks the others' stout body plates; but it, too, is different from the "leiurus" form of the British three-spined stickleback.

All four types are now regarded as subspecies of a single species—*Gasterosteus aculeatus*—but this could change.

Two other species of *Gasterosteus* are also known, but one—*G. crenobiontus* from Romania—has become extinct and was officially listed in 1997. The other is far from extinct. It is the 3-inch (7.5-cm) blackspotted stickleback (*G. wheatlandi*) that occurs in brackish and marine habitats along the Atlantic coastline of eastern Canada and the U.S. from Newfoundland down to Massachusetts. It has been known to enter fresh water, but only rarely, and is found mostly in near-shore areas among vegetation. It is reported that this species lives for only a year, but the three-spined (*G. aculeatus*) lives for three and the nine-spined (*Pungitius pungitius pungitius*) for five.

## The Nine-spines

The nine-spined stickleback (*Pungitius pungitius*) may not have nine spines but from six to twelve, so its common name is not really appropriate. Neither is its most widely used alternative name—the ten-spined stickleback. It is one of two subspecies of *P. pungitius* that currently is given the full name of *Pungitius pungitius pungitius*—to distinguish it from *P. p. tymensis*, a smaller, 2.8-inch (7-cm) version found in Japan and the Russian Federation. *P. p. pungitius* is 3.5 inches (9 cm) long.

This Japanese-Russian nine-spined is called the Sakhalin stickleback because of its Russian distribution. It is strictly a freshwater fish, but its more widely distributed relative is also found in fresh, brackish, and fully marine waters. Like the three-spined stickleback, *P. p. pungitius* occurs on both sides of the Atlantic—in the west from Canada down to New Jersey; in the east, all the main drainages of northern Europe and Asia stretching from the U.K. to Korea, Japan, and China. It is also found on the Pacific coast of Alaska and in the Great Lakes basin.

Like the three-spined stickleback, the Amur stickleback (*P. sinensis sinensis*) is interesting in that it grows to different sizes in different habitats—in fresh water it only grows to 2.6 inches (6.5 cm), but in sea water it can reach 3.5 inches (9 cm) in length. The little-known subspecies of the Amur stickleback—(*P. sinensis kaibarae*)—is restricted to freshwater habitats in parts of Japan.

The smoothtail nine-spined stickleback (*P. laevis*), a freshwater species, occurs in England and France; little is known about its life history.

The southern nine-spined stickleback (*P. platygaster*) is a widely distributed European and Asian species that grows to around 2.8 inches (7 cm); it is highly adaptable in its habitats, found in fresh, brackish, and marine waters. Its smaller Central Asian closest relative is the Aral stickleback (*P. platygaster aralensis*), found mostly in the Aral Sea. Almost the smallest stickleback, it measures just 2.1 inches (5.3 cm) in length; it is restricted to freshwater habitats, stretching over a wide part of its Central Asian range, where it is found, largely, in lakes and gentle-flowing bodies of water.

## Contrasting North Americans

Two North American sticklebacks look very like the three-spined stickleback—the four-spined stickleback (*Apeltes quadracus*) and the brook

*Like all sticklebacks, this nine-spined stickleback (Pungitius pungitius) swims in its preferred habitat of vegetation with little water movement. Its mouth open, it will eat mostly invertebrates, but also fish eggs, larvae, and small fish.*

stickleback (*Culaea inconstans*), with three to five spines and four to six spines, respectively.

In the four-spined the dorsal spines are angled in relation to each other, slanting alternately to right and left, with the first two longer than the rest. During the breeding season mature, 2.5-inch (6.4-cm) black males look spectacular—they develop red pelvic fins.

This predominantly marine species occurs near coasts from Canada's Gulf of St. Lawrence to the coastal strip of North Carolina. It is often found in weedy areas and will enter brackish water but rarely into fully freshwater habitats.

In marked contrast, the brook stickleback is a freshwater species that rarely ventures into brackish water but never into the sea. It likes cool, quiet, vegetated waters in ponds, lakes, and backwaters in the northern half of North America. It occurs as far north as the Northwest Territories of the Arctic drainage, spreading south to the Great Lakes and Mississippi River basin, into Montana, southern Ohio, and Nebraska, and east as far as Nova Scotia.

There is also an isolated population in part of the Canadian River that runs through New Mexico—a prime example of the situation mentioned earlier in which the three-spined stickleback could evolve into a new species or subspecies of brook stickleback. Changes are already taking place elsewhere in

## Threatened Stickleback

Somewhat better known than some of its closest relatives—but partly for the wrong reasons—is the Greek nine-spined (or ten-spined) stickleback (*P. hellenicus*).

This slender species only grows to around 2 inches (5 cm), and most unusually for a stickleback, it does not have any spines at all! It is a secretive species that lives among the vegetated edges of springs and small rivers in the Sperchios River basin in the central parts of eastern Greece. It is said to bury itself in the bottom mud when escaping from predators.

Unfortunately for this tiny species, its water is also needed by our own species, and as almost invariably happens in such unequal contests, the stickleback is losing out. In fact, its position is so much under threat (it is believed to be now extinct in some parts of its restricted range) that it is officially listed by the World Conservation Union as Critically Endangered.

this species' range, with the population in Alberta and Saskatchewan lacking pelvic fins.

### Ultraslim Giant

The largest member of the entire family is the fifteen-spined stickleback (*Spinachia spinachia*)—also called the sea stickleback—which can grow to around 9 inches (23 cm). An eastern Atlantic species, it occurs close to shore along coasts stretching from northern Norway southward to the northern parts of the Bay of Biscay, as well as in the Baltic Sea.

It is an extremely elongated, slim fish with a sharply pointed snout and a very long, thin caudal peduncle. As in most other sticklebacks, the number of spines along the back varies—in this case from 14 to 17. Also just like its relatives, it is the male that builds the nest, often in tidal pools; it consists of seaweed stuck together. Like the nine-spined stickleback, the fifteen-spine builds its nest clear of the bottom.

A single female may lay up to 200 eggs; then, in sharp contrast to other stickleback species, the female dies. The male guards the eggs in typically vigorous fashion.

Short dragonfish (*Eurypegasus draconis*)

**Common name** Seamoths

**Family** Pegasidae

**Order** Gasterosteiformes

**Number of species** 5 in 2 genera

**Size** From 3.7 in (9.5 cm) to 7 in (18 cm)

**Key features** Body broad and flattened, encased in bony plates; front of head narrower, with prominent eyes; long, flattened, pointed snout; mouth small, located on underside of tip of snout; dorsal and anal fins short; pectoral fins large and winglike; pelvic fins with 1 long spine and few soft rays; tail small, but tail section long and squarish, with projections along its length; coloration variable: mottled brown with overlying netlike pattern to pale to mottled gray; some species capable of color changes; juveniles often differently colored than adults

**Breeding** Pairs rise off bottom, pressing abdomens (bellies) together and releasing eggs and sperm about 40 in (1 m) above the bottom; eggs float and hatch just over a day later

**Diet** Small invertebrates, usually sucked in from surface of muddy, silty, sandy, or rubbly bottom

**Habitat** Predominantly marine, but 3 species enter brackish estuaries; usually found at depths of less than 295 ft (90 m); 1 species found at depths of 260–950 ft (80–290 m); rubbly, sandy, silty, or muddy bottoms; sometimes partly buried

**Distribution** Tropical and temperate regions of Indo-West Pacific

**Status** World Conservation Union lists brick seamoth (*Pegasus laternarius*) as Vulnerable because of actual or potential levels of harvesting or changes in habitat; concern about other 4 species, but data unavailable

⊕ *The pelvic fin spines and rays, together with its midbrown color, help camouflage this 4-inch (10-cm) short dragonfish (Eurypegasus draconis)—also called the dwarf seamoth—on the sandy or silty bottoms that it inhabits.*

# Seamoths

Pegasidae

*Gliding over a rubbly bottom on winglike pectoral fins, the dwarf seamoth looks very much like some of its terrestrial namesakes, but with a long snout. Sadly, seamoths remain under threat in the wild.*

ALONG WITH ITS FOUR CLOSEST relatives the dwarf seamoth is a member of the family Pegasidae from the Indo-Pacific. Their unusual features include a hard body armor consisting of bony plates, a very long, pointed, but flattened snout, and a flattened (depressed) body.

Seamoths resemble sea horses (family Syngnathidae) with their body armor and pointed snouts. However, their depressed body, allied to the presence of pelvic fins and a breeding strategy in which pairs rise from the bottom to release their eggs and sperm into the water, make them very different. In contrast, sea horses have compressed (flattened) bodies, and males brood their eggs in a belly pouch.

## Secretive Seamoth

Though various species of seamoth have been seen and photographed, relatively few details are known about their biology.

Seamoths eat small invertebrates, picked up directly from the bottom, so they do not dig for their food. Some species, such as the sculptured seamoth (*Pegasus lancifer*) and the slender, or longtail, seamoth (*P. volitans*), also called the winged dragonfish, bury themselves in sandy, silty, or muddy bottoms and change color to match their surroundings. While color changes may not be possible in all species, some, like the dwarf seamoth and the brick seamoth (*P. laternarius*), occur in various colors.

As they swim, seamoths extend their large, winglike pectoral fins to glide over the bottom. They can also walk, using their pelvic fins.

Courtship and mating usually occur during the spring, with most activity taking place at dusk during the largest tides. Males use their large pectorals, often decorated with splashes of color, to entice a female to spawn. If this is

⊖ *These male and female slender seamoths (Pegasus volitans) form one of five species in the family Pegasidae. The others are the sculptured seamoth (P. lancifer), brick seamoth (P. laternarius), dwarf seamoth (Eurypegasus draconis), and Hawaiian seamoth (E. papilio). All species display their distinctive rayed and winglike pectoral fins.*

successful, the pair rise away from the bottom with their bellies pressed close to each other and shed their eggs and sperm into the water.

Fertilized eggs float to the surface, where they hatch in a day or so. The larvae may spend some time swimming and feeding among the plankton; then they drop gradually to the bottom. It is not known if this is true for every species or how long the developmental stages take. For example, in the case of the Hawaiian seamoth (*Eurypegasus papilio*) larvae and juveniles are frequently netted in midwater, while the adults occur on the bottom at depths of between 260 and 950 feet (80–290 m).

## Skin "Jumping"

Few fish shed their skin, at least in significant quantities. Even fewer change their whole skin in a single "jump." But seamoths are not ordinary fish. A dwarf seamoth specimen, kept in an aquarium, was observed performing this action precisely—with photographic evidence.

The specimen was covered in algae and small invertebrates, not an unusual situation for a slow, bottom-living fish. Apparently, the seamoth shed its whole skin in a single piece by what can only be described as "jumping out of it"—in one rapid movement to rid itself of its accumulated load of irritants. However, scientists do not know if this is a regular occurrence, or whether other members of the family ever do the same thing.

Armored stickleback (*Indostomus paradoxus*)

**Common name** Sea horses, pipefish, and allies

**Families**   Syngnathidae (sea horses, pipefish, pipehorses, seadragons), Solenostomidae (ghost pipefish), Indostomidae (armored sticklebacks)

**Subfamilies** Syngnathidae: Syngnathinae (pipefish, pipehorses, seadragons); Hippocampinae (sea horses)

**Order**   Gasterosteiformes

**Number of species** Syngnathidae: around 270 in 52 genera; Solenostomidae: 4 in 1 genus; Indostomidae: 3 in 1 genus

**Size**   From 0.95 in (2.4 cm) to 37.4 in (95 cm)

**Key features** Elongated body (encased in bony rings or star-shaped plates): held upright (sea horses), or horizontal (pipefish, seadragons); long snout (short in armored sticklebacks), small mouth; 1 to 2 dorsal fins, some with spines and soft rays; some species lack pelvic, caudal, anal fins; long, slim caudal peduncle (armored sticklebacks); varied coloration: muted browns to bright colors; sometimes patterned body or dark bars on fins

**Breeding**   Male carries eggs in belly pouch or mass of spongy tissue (sea horses); female carries eggs in pouch formed by pelvic fin (ghost pipefish)

**Diet**   Invertebrates, worms, and other bottom-dwellers

**Habitat**   Shallow coral reefs, seagrass meadows above 165 ft (50 m) depth or to 310 ft (95 m); some in brackish estuaries; armored sticklebacks in still or slow-moving fresh water, leaf litter on bottom

**Distribution** Widely distributed in tropical, subtropical, and warm temperate regions of Atlantic, Indian, and Pacific Oceans, and Indo-West Pacific; also Myanmar, Cambodia, Thailand, Mekong Basin

**Status**   World Conservation Union lists 45 sea horse and pipefish species as under threat; sea horse species: 19 Vulnerable, 1 Endangered; pipefish species: 5 Vulnerable, 1 Critically Endangered

⊕ *This 1.2-inch (3-cm) long armored stickleback (**Indostomus paradoxus**) can leap out of the water.*

# Sea Horses, Pipefish, and Allies

Syngnathidae, Solenostomidae, Indostomidae

*We call sea horses quaint and delightful and often do not even think of them as fish. Yet they are beautiful examples of evolution, resulting in creatures ideally adapted to their environment.*

SEA HORSES DO NOT LOOK LIKE FISH AT ALL. THEY STAND upright in water, their head at the top and tail at the bottom. In the closely related pipefish the head is at the front and the tail at the back. In sea horses the head points forward, as in normal fish, so that it sits at right angles on top of the body rather than in line with it.

**Unfishlike Fish**

These are not the only unfishlike characteristics that these remarkable creatures have. The tail, for example, does not have a fin but is a long, rounded extension of the body (the caudal peduncle), used to hold on to plants, just like monkeys on land. Sea horses do not have pelvic fins, and their small pectoral fins look like ears; their long snout makes them look horselike, hence their name. The single dorsal fin has flexible rays and is located halfway down the body, pointing backward (not upward as with other fish). They use this fin for swimming; it acts like a caudal fin in more conventional fish.

Sea horses have bony plates, not scales, on their bodies—a protective body armor that makes sea horses hard-to-swallow prey. In atypical fashion it is the male sea horses that become pregnant and give birth, not the females. Sea horses are truly unfishlike fish.

**Not-so-faithful Breeders**

It was thought sea horses paired for life, but loyalty only exists between some pairs depending on species and other factors; in the pot-bellied sea horse (*Hippocampus abdominalis*) there is little loyalty, for example.

⊙ *Like all sea horses, this colorful slender sea horse (Hippocampus reidi) has the typical pronounced snout, small mouth, and upright position in the water. Sea horses acquired their name from the horselike appearance of the snout.*

# Record-breaking Discovery

**D**epending on which classification or book is consulted, there are as few as 32 species of sea horse—or as many as 120. To them must now be added a new one that was described in 2003.

It is Denise's pygmy sea horse (*Hippocampus denise*)—a record-breaker in that it is the smallest sea horse species known to science. Fully grown males measure just 0.9 inches (2.2 cm), with females being only slightly larger, about 0.95 inches (2.4 cm). Sexual maturity can be reached when the fish are only 0.6 inches (1.6 cm) in length.

According to its discoverer, zoologist Sara Lourie (who also codescribed the species with J.E. Randall), this tiny species lives deeper within coral heads than most other species, which could help its survival in the wild. It is also a more active species than other small sea horses, which makes its name "Denise" most appropriate, since it is derived from the Greek and means "wild or frenzied."

*The World Conservation Union has classified the Knysna sea horse (Hippocampus capensis) as Endangered. It occurs in the Knysna Lagoon west of Port Elizabeth, South Africa.*

When courting begins between a potential breeding pair, the female looks fuller than the male—he then develops a swollen belly pouch to show his readiness to mate. After a graceful display of "dancing" and entwining of tails, the pair face each other and bring their bellies close together. As the male opens the top of his abdominal pouch, the female transfers some eggs into it, and then he fertilizes them.

Depending on age, size, and species, a female can produce up to 1,570 eggs (usually considerably fewer, often less than 100), which the male incubates. Two to four weeks later he gives birth, a process that can last up to 12 hours or more.

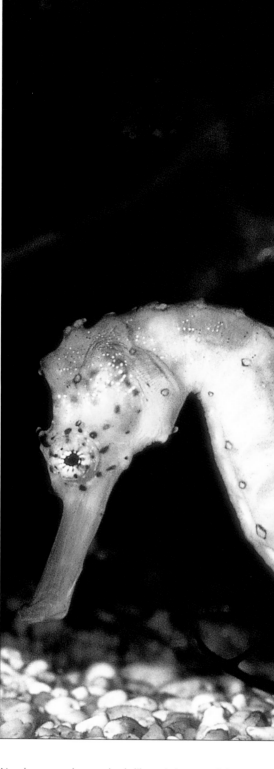

Newborn sea horses look like miniature adults. They are totally ignored by their father, so they have to fend for themselves from the start.

## Similar, but Different

In their closest relatives—pipefish, pipehorses, and seadragons—the males also brood their eggs in special belly pouches, or spongy tissue under the tail, eventually giving birth.

However, in the pipefish the body is aligned in the more conventional way, with the head and snout directed forward, the tail directed backward, and the dorsal fin directed upward. In the seadragons (such as *Pycodorus* and *Phyllopteryx*) and the pipehorses (such as *Solegnathus* species) frequently the head and tail are held at an angle that lies somewhere between a sea horse and a pipefish.

Both the seadragons and pipefish have the same sort of snout that sea horses have. They also lack pelvic fins, and their pectoral fins lie close to the head and, in many species, have the appearance of ears. Along with other features, such as body casing, this means that currently pipefish, pipehorses, seadragons, and sea horses are all regarded as members of a single family (Syngnathidae) but belonging to

⬆ *A pair of long-snouted sea horses (*Hippocampus guttulatus*) perform their graceful courtship display by "dancing" and entwining their tails.*

# Seaweed-imitating Dragons

There are three members of the pipefish that bear no resemblance to their other relatives. In fact, one looks so much like a clump of floating seaweed that it is frequently impossible to clarify that it is a fish at all. Indeed, the camouflage of the leafy seadragon (*Phycodurus eques*) is so effective that neither its predators nor its prey are even aware of its presence. Therefore predators miss a possible meal, while prey do not know that they are being hunted until it is too late.

The weedy seadragon (*Phyllopteryx taeniolatus*) also gives a good impression of a seaweed, but perhaps not quite so effectively—although its young are next to impossible to spot among bottom vegetation. The ribboned seadragon (*Haliichthys taeniophorus*) looks a little like a very slim, nonupright sea horse with tufts of seaweed growing out of its body. Of the three seadragon species it is the least developed (in terms of leafy growths) and, at 12 inches (30 cm) in length, probably looks more like a single, long frond of seaweed than a clump.

Like all members of the family Syngathidae, the seadragons are male brooders. The eggs are embedded in soft, spongy tissue that runs from just below the belly along the lower edge of the caudal peduncle. A large male can carry up to 300 eggs for up to eight weeks. When the young hatch, they look more or less like miniature replicas of their parents, and they are able to fend for themselves after the first few hours. Both the leafy and weedy seadragons have been bred in captivity.

two separate subfamilies—Syngnathinae (pipefish, pipehorses, and seadragons) and Hippocampinae (sea horses). However, this situation may change after further study.

## Ghostly Relatives

Closely related to both the sea horses and the pipefish are the ghost pipefish, which make up the family Solenostomidae. There are only five species in the family, ranging in size from about 2.4 inches (6 cm) in the armored pipefish (*Solenostomus armatus*) to 6.7 inches (17 cm) in "the" ghost pipefish (*S. cyanopterus*).

Like their namesakes, the pipefish, *Solenostomus* species, hold their bodies in the normal way—that is, horizontal, with their head pointing forward and their tail back. However, they can be easily separated from the other pipefish because they have two dorsal fins, a large tail, and large pelvic fins. As a result, they are better swimmers than their

relatives. Their body armor, too, is different and consists of large, star-shaped bony plates.

The pelvic fins (totally lacking in sea horses and pipefish) serve a very important purpose in the ghost pipefish. In females they form a pouch in which she carries her eggs until they hatch. However, in the sea horses and pipefish the developing eggs are carried in the belly pouches of the males.

was no dispute. The actual relationship of this family to other armored fish families has been hotly contested for years, however. Even its scientific name reflects this—"paradoxus"—a paradox being something that is contradictory or apparently absurd, but that may be true.

The discovery and subsequent naming of two further species in 1999 did little to resolve the situation. And so the controversy carries on to this day. Most scientists take the view that the three armored sticklebacks belong within the same order as the sticklebacks, along with sea horses, pipefish, seadragons, and ghost pipefish, but in a group of their own—the infraorder Indostomoida.

These elongated, slender fish only measure around 1.2 inches (3 cm) in length; but unlike their relatives, which are all marine, they are restricted to fresh water. They are shy, retiring fish that inhabit still or slowly flowing waters. They spend most of their time hiding and hunting in the thick layers of leaf litter that line the bottom of streams, lakes, ditches, canals, and swamps, where they feed on small, slow-moving invertebrates such as worms.

One species—"the" armored stickleback—is known primarily from Lake Indawgyi in Myanmar (formerly Burma) but may also extend into Cambodia. *Indostomus crocodilus* (no common name) is known only from a blackwater stream in Narathiwat Province, Thailand, while *I. spinosus* (no common name) has a wider distribution in the Mekong Basin.

Very little is known about the biology and, particularly, the breeding habits of these intriguing little fish, although the armored stickleback occasionally is available for home aquariums. Thanks to this some important information has emerged over the years. We know, for example, that this species is among the very few fish that can actually raise and lower its head. We also know that it frequently rests on the bottom with its body aligned at a steep, upward angle, and that it creeps up on worms—using its pectoral fins to move forward and then turning at very fast speed to snap up its prey.

## Controversial Sticklebacks

In the world of family relationships fish are no different than other animals or even humans. Sometimes scientists argue about how different species are related. The armored stickleback (*Indostomus paradoxus*) is an excellent example of such a debate.

Until 1999 it was the only known member of its family (Indostomidae)—of this fact there

⇡ *At 6.7 inches (17 cm) long the ornate ghost pipefish (*Solenostomus paradoxus*) is the largest species in the family Solenostomidae. It inhabits the shallow coral reefs in Indonesia.*

⊖ *This male leafy seadragon (Phycodurus eques) displays the leafy growths typical of its genus. They provide very effective camouflage as it hunts for prey in coral reefs near Kangaroo Island, Australia.*

⊕ *This red-and-yellow banded pipefish (Dunckerocampus pessuliferus) swims in the normal horizontal position, with head pointing forward and tail back. This male (in Indonesian waters) is carrying eggs in a belly pouch on his abdomen.*

## The Sea-horse Trade

Although it is difficult, perhaps impossible, to state accurately just how many sea horses are caught and traded worldwide, it is safe to say that the figure is over 15 million each year. Sea horses are fished, both as targeted species (that is, they are specifically sought out and collected) or as bycatch (that is, they are caught accidentally in nets set out for other fish). Either way, for many years now there has been mounting concern for the continued survival of at least some species of sea horses, pipefish, and pipehorses in the wild.

There are three main markets for sea horses—traditional Chinese medicine (TCM), ornaments (or curios), and home aquaria. Of them the TCM market is the largest by far, with dried sea horses being sold either whole or in powdered form. Whole sea horses are generally used in tonics and other health-associated drinks, while powdered sea horses are used in a wide variety of medicines designed to treat numerous ailments and illnesses—from asthma to thickening of the arteries or even for broken bones.

These popular remedies have spread around the world, and they now are sold outside China in countries such as the Philippines, Indonesia, India, the U.S., U.K., and other countries that have an Asian expatriate community. It has been estimated that across Asia some 45 tons (40.8 tonnes) of dried sea

# Sea Horses Under Threat

Together the 45 or so countries that trade in sea horses account for between 3 and 15 tons (2.7–13.6 tonnes) of fish every year. This translates into many millions of individual specimens and has led to concern about their status in the wild. No fewer than 19 are now officially listed as Vulnerable by the World Conservation Union, and one—the Knysna, or Cape, sea horse (*Hippocampus capensis*)—is considered Endangered. (Below are sea horses (*Hippocampus* species) for sale for traditional Chinese medicine use in Sabah, Malaysia.)

Among the pipefish five species of *Solegnathus* are also listed as Vulnerable, while the river pipefish (*Syngnathus watermeyeri*) is Critically Endangered.

In the case of the Knysna sea horse, which is found west of Port Elizabeth in Cape Province, South Africa, tourism and pollution have put the species at risk. Tourism is responsible for creating pressure on the estuary around Knysna Lagoon, where freshwater floods have caused heavy die-offs among the resident sea-horse population (these sea horses cannot tolerate low salinity). Increasing levels of pollution also mean that even captive-bred specimens cannot be released into the waters, so restocking is not possible. However, if attempts to control conditions in the natural habitat are successful, the release of captive-bred specimens may be possible in the future.

The situation facing the river pipefish is even worse. This species is restricted to tidal areas of just three South African rivers: Kariega, Kasouga, and Bushman's. This extremely small distribution means that the species is at high risk from external influences like pollution, flooding, loss of its seagrass-bed habitat, or disease. Furthermore, this pipefish appears to have a very short breeding season. Therefore anything that upsets weather or water conditions during this time could pose a threat to the survival of the species.

horses are imported annually. In terms of actual numbers of specimens this probably represents over 15 million individual sea horses.

Large numbers are also sold as curios or ornaments, mainly (but not exclusively) in vacation areas near the sea. Sea horses of all sizes are used and sold—incorporated into anything from a keyring to a lamp base.

In contrast, live sea horses are mainly destined for home aquaria. Past estimates suggest that many hundreds of thousands were caught specifically for this purpose. However, studies carried out in recent years indicate that the numbers are more likely to be a few tens of thousands; this does not mean that only these numbers are caught alive. Many more may be collected and subsequently sold for TCM and curio purposes.

In a global attempt to protect all species of sea horse the Convention in International Trade in Endangered Species of Fauna and Flora—known as CITES—agreed in the fall of 2002 to put all *Hippocampus* species on their Appendix II list. This agreement came into effect on May 15, 2004, which means that special permits have been required to sell and buy sea horses since this date. It is not a ban on trade, but it does mean that trade in these species is now monitored and controlled.

A further and important development in recent years is the considerable increase in the numbers of sea horses being bred in captivity especially for the marine hobbyist. Many thousands of these captive-bred sea horses (consisting of several species) are now being produced in a number of countries, including Australia, Ireland, and the U.K., for sale worldwide. Therefore the future of sea horses now appears to be more promising, although the problem of large numbers being caught accidentally still continues.

↪ *Here in waters off southeast Australia a "pregnant" male short-snouted sea horse (*Hippocampus breviceps*), carries his eggs in a belly pouch. In two to four weeks' time he will give birth to live young, a process that lasts up to 12 hours or more.*

Chinese trumpetfish (*Aulostomus chinensis*)

**Common name** Trumpetfish and cornetfish

**Families** Aulostomidae (trumpetfish),
Fistulariidae (cornetfish)

**Order** Gasterosteiformes

**Number of species** Aulostomidae: 3 in 1 genus;
Fistulariidae: 4 in 1 genus

**Size** From around 27.5 in (70 cm) to 6.6 ft (2 m)

**Key features** Extremely elongated body with scales
(trumpetfish), naked, or with pricklelike scutes
(cornetfish); long heads and snouts (shorter in
trumpetfish with single central snout barbel);
isolated dorsal spines (trumpetfish); tail either
rounded (trumpetfish) or forked with central
filament (cornetfish); coloration variable, capable
of changing; usually greenish or brownish on
back, fading to white along belly, with or
without body spotting

**Breeding** Spawning mainly in spring or summer; eggs
scattered in open water, then abandoned;
hatching takes several days

**Diet** Mainly small fish and invertebrates

**Habitat** Usually associated with reefs but found over
range of bottoms; shallow to deeper water

**Distribution** Tropical and subtropical regions of Indo-Pacific,
Eastern Pacific, and Atlantic Oceans

⊕ *The 31-inch (80-cm) Chinese trumpetfish (Aulostomus
chinensis) lives in the clear, shallow water of coral reefs
throughout the Indo-Pacific. It uses both stealth and camouflage
to catch unsuspecting prey, like small fish and shrimp.*

# Trumpetfish and Cornetfish
Aulostomidae, Fistulariidae

*A cornet is very similar to a trumpet, but it is more
tapered in its overall shape. Likewise, a cornetfish is
very similar to a trumpetfish, but as with its musical
instrument counterpart, it is more tapered.*

THE MORE TAPERED EFFECT IN CORNETFISH (family
Fistulariidae) is largely produced by a long
filament that grows out of the center of the
tail. The filament itself consists of the tail's two
middle rays and can be almost as long as the
stretched-out, tubelike head of these fish. In
the trumpetfish (family Aulostomidae) there is
no caudal filament; the head, although
stretched out and tubelike, is not quite so long.

## Trumpets and Cornets Compared

Other than the tail filament being present or
absent and the tubelike mouth's relative length,
there are several features that make it possible
to separate a trumpetfish from a cornetfish.

Trumpetfish have a barbel (whisker) on the
tip of the lower jaw and a compressed body,
while cornetfish do not have a barbel, and the
body is depressed. Trumpetfish also have scales,
but cornetfish are either naked or have tiny
pricklelike plates (scutes) arranged in several
rows along the body.

They also have different dorsal fins. In the
trumpetfish the soft dorsal (containing 22 to 27
rays) is preceded by a row of 8 to 12 small,
isolated spines—absent in the cornetfish, whose
soft dorsal contains between 13 and 20 rays.
In addition, the caudal (tail) fin is rounded in
the trumpetfish but forked in the cornetfish
with the added central filament.

Less easily seen, the anus is located a long
way behind the pelvic fins in the trumpetfish
but is close to them in the cornetfish. Internally
the shorter-bodied trumpetfish have 59 to 64
individual vertebrae (back bones), compared to
76 to 87 in cornetfish.

⊕ *The Caribbean
trumpetfish (Aulostomus
maculatus) is also called
a trumpeter. At 40 inches
(1 m) long it is the
largest trumpetfish and
occurs in shallow waters
of the western Atlantic
at depths down to
80 feet (25 m).*

Although trumpetfish and cornetfish look superficially similar, they are sufficiently distinct to form totally separate families—Aulostomidae and Fistulariidae, respectively.

### Stealth Hunters

Trumpetfish stay close to coral reefs either to gain protection by following shoaling fish or as a way to get near potential prey. They are called "stealth hunters"—often "floating" toward unsuspecting prey in a head-down position resembling a strand of seaweed. When close enough, they make a downward dart at their prey (a crab, shrimp, or small fish) and suck it in with their long, tubelike mouth.

Cornetfish also ambush their prey but are not as well camouflaged as trumpetfish, nor can they change color. However, they swim faster, so can chase their prey in open water. Their exceptionally long snout also allows them to suck out prey from among coral growths.

### Size and Range

There are just three species of trumpetfish, and all are tropical in origin. The confusingly named Atlantic cornetfish (*Aulostomus strigosus*) is not a cornetfish but a trumpetfish. It is found in shallow waters at around 80 feet (25 m) in the eastern Atlantic and, at 29.5 inches (75 cm), is the smallest of the trumpetfish. The largest is the trumpeter, or Caribbean trumpetfish (*A. maculatus*), around 40 inches (1 m), also found at similar depths but in the western Atlantic.

Along with the third species—the 31.5-inch (80-cm) Chinese trumpetfish (*A. chinensis*)—the trumpeter is fished commercially, usually for local markets. There is also a yellow form of the Chinese trumpetfish, which is the one most commonly seen in public aquaria. In the wild this species occurs down to 400 feet (122 m).

There are only four species of cornetfish, all in one genus—*Fistularia*. The 27.6-inch (70-cm) Pacific cornetfish (*F. corneta*) is the smallest species (smaller than the smallest trumpetfish), but the other three are all larger. Two of them—the red cornetfish (*F. petimba*) and "the" cornetfish (*F. tabacaria*)—grow to 6.6 feet (2 m) and range down to a depth of 655 feet (200 m). All four cornetfish are sold fresh, dried, salted, smoked, or are ground into fishmeal, but all the fisheries are small and aimed primarily at local markets.

As its name implies, the Pacific cornetfish occurs in the eastern Pacific, while the wide-ranging bluespotted cornetfish (*F. commersonii*) is found in both the eastern Pacific and the Indo-Pacific. The two remaining species—the red cornetfish and the cornetfish—are found on both sides of the Atlantic, although the red cornetfish also extends into the Indo-Pacific. They are also known to enter brackish estuaries.

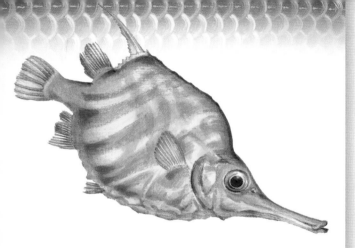

Banded yellowfish (*Centriscops humerosus*)

**Common name** Snipefish, shrimpfish, and relatives

**Family**      Centriscidae

**Subfamilies** Centriscinae, Macroramphinae

**Order**       Gasterosteiformes

**Number of species** 13 in 5 genera

**Size**        From 6 in (15 cm) to 13.4 in (34 cm)

**Key features** Body from long and slim (razorfish) to deep (snipefish, bellowfish); extended snout; eyes relatively large; body encased in bony plates that form sharp edge along back (snipefish, bellowfish), also belly (razorfish); first dorsal fin has 1 long spine and several short ones directed backward in line with back or upward; second dorsal and caudal fin displaced at downward angle (razorfish) but lined up more "normally" (snipefish, bellowfish); coloration: silvery with variable lengthwise banding (razorfish); more brilliant coloration, with red, violet, or brown oblique body bands (bellowfish, snipefish)

**Breeding**   Few details available; eggs scattered, then abandoned to float among plankton, where larvae spend some time before migrating toward midwater or bottom

**Diet**         Small invertebrates, including zooplankton

**Habitat**    Shallow to very shallow waters (usually reefs) in tropical regions but may also occur in deeper waters; also some in temperate waters

**Distribution** Atlantic, Indian, and Pacific Oceans

⊕ *The extended snout of the 10-inch (25-cm) banded yellowfish (Centriscops humerosus) is typical of the family Centriscidae. This fish is found at depths between 115 and 3,280 feet (35–1,000 m).*

# Snipefish and Shrimpfish

Centriscidae

*Some snipefish look more like floating razors than "true" fish, with their pointed snouts and sharp-edged bellies. No wonder these knife-edge imitators are also known as razorfish.*

FOUR OF THE 13 SPECIES in the family Centriscidae fit this description to a certain extent and are members of the genera *Aeoliscus* and *Centriscus*. Seven other species (members of two genera, *Centriscops* and *Notopogon*) are much more deep-bodied but still retain the long, slender snout. The two *Macroramphosus* species fall between the other two groups.

## Shrimp or Razors?

For a small family the different genera and species have a large number of common names. For example, one species of *Aeoliscus* (*A. punctulatus*) is a shrimpfish, while the other (*A. strigatus*) is a razorfish, along with two species of *Centriscus*. The two *Macroramphosus* species are called snipefish, while the single *Centriscops* (*C. humerosus*) is a yellowfish. Six bellowfish species are in the genus *Notopogon*.

All the common names have explanations. Although the shrimpfish neither looks like a shrimp nor is associated, its back is covered in sharply pointed plates, ending in a long, sharp dorsal fin spine, which feel like a shrimp's back. The term "razorfish" refers to the razorlike bottom edge of the body of some species. Snipefish are named because of their long, pointed snout—a snipe is a bird with a long, straight, pointed beak. Bellowfish resemble bellows (contraptions that blow air onto a fire).

Yellowfish may be an old misspelling of bellowfish that has been retained, since the yellowfish is not yellow—it is orange with dark bands—and looks very much like a bellowfish. However, the bellowfish's orange coloration may have been seen as a deep yellow.

⊕ *The grooved razorfish (Centriscus scutatus) is also called the speckled shrimpfish or razorfish. This fish and the slender snipefish (Macroramphosus gracilis) are the smallest members in the family Centriscidae—at only 6 inches (15 cm) long.*

## Prickly Associations

The two species of *Aeoliscus* form close associations with sea urchins, particularly the long-spined sea urchin (*Diadema*). They use the venom-tipped spines of the urchins as an extremely successful form of protection, diving headfirst among them at the first sign of danger. They also use the spaces between long-branched corals, such as staghorn coral (*Acropora*), in a similar way.

In the speckled shrimpfish (*A. punctulatus*) individuals of all ages engage in this behavior. In the closely related razorfish (*A. strigatus*), while adults may also dive among sea urchin spines or coral branches, individuals or shoals can also be found sheltering head-down in strands of seagrass or whip corals.

Whichever option is chosen, the unusual evasive or protective action taken by these fish is highly effective; large schools of both exist wherever sea urchins and corals occur.

## Bellows and Spines

The bellowfish look quite different overall than their slim razor-edged relatives. They are deep-bodied fish that do not form any kind of association with sea urchins, corals, or any other organisms. They have several dorsal spines, the second of which is very long, strong, and sharply pointed.

Because of the bellowfish's overall shape their second dorsal fin, which only contains soft rays, is located on the upper part of the body, although set well back and near the tail. However, in the razorfish the soft second dorsal is placed below the first dorsal, slotted right at the end of the body—the prominent spine points backward rather than upward. As a result, the second dorsal fin faces backward and slightly downward—perfect for fish that spend most of their lives standing on their heads.

These features make it relatively simple to separate the bellowfish and their immediate relatives from the razorfish and their own immediate relatives. They help explain why a fish like a longspine snipefish (*Macroramphosus scolopax*) belongs with the bellowfish rather than the razorfish, despite the fact that it does not have the deep body that is characteristic of the bellowfish. Bellowfish also inhabit much deeper water than razorfish; they frequently occur at depths well over 1,970 feet (600 m).

# Mail-cheeked Fish Order Scorpaeniformes

## Order Scorpaeniformes: 7 suborders, 25 families, 260 genera, around 1,326 species

**Suborder** Dactylopteroidei—1 family, 2 genera, and 7 species

**Family** Dactylopteridae—flying or helmet gurnards

**Suborder** Scorpaenoidei—7 families, about 92 genera, and 590 species

**Families** Scorpaenidae—scorpionfish*; Caracanthidae—orbicular velvetfish; Aploactinidae—velvetfish; Pataecidae—Australian prowfish; Gnathanacanthidae—red velvetfish; Congiopodidae—pigfish, horsefish, or racehorses; Triglidae—gurnards or sea robins**

\* THE SCORPAENIDAE ARE DIVIDED BY NELSON 1994 (SEE BIBLIOGRAPHY) INTO 11 SUBFAMILIES; SOME OF THEM ARE REGARDED AS FULL FAMILIES BY OTHER SCIENTISTS (SEE ENTRY FOR SCORPIONFISH FOR FULL BREAKDOWN)

\*\* THE TRIGLIDAE ARE SUBDIVIDED INTO 2 SUBFAMILIES BY NELSON 1994:

- TRIGLINAE—GURNARDS OR SEAROBINS

- PERISTEDINAE—ARMORED GURNARDS OR ARMORED SEA ROBINS

THESE SUBFAMILIES ARE REGARDED AS FULL FAMILIES BY SOME AUTHORS (SEE ENTRY FOR GURNARDS FOR FULLER DETAILS)

**Suborder** Platycephaloidei (3 families, about 22 genera, and 85 species)

**Families** Bembridae—deepwater flatheads; Platycephalidae—flatheads; Hoplichthyidae—ghost flatheads

**Suborder** Anoplopomatoidei—1 family, 1 genus, and 2 species

**Family** Anoplomatidae—sablefish

**Suborder** Hexagrammoidei—1 family, 5 genera, and 11 species

**Family** Hexagrammidae—greenlings, lingcod, combfish, and allies*

\*THE HEXAGRAMMIDAE ARE DIVIDED INTO 5 SUBFAMILIES (SEE ENTRY FOR GREENLINGS AND ALLIES FOR BREAKDOWN AND FULLER DETAILS)

**Suborder** Normanichthyiodei—1 family, 1 genus, and 1 species

**Family** Normanichthyidae

**Suborder** Cottoidei—11 families, about 137 genera, and over 630 species

**Families** Rhamphocottidae—grunt sculpin; Ereuniidae; Cottidae—sculpins; Comephoridae—Baikal oilfish; Abyssocottidae; Hemitripteridae; Agonidae—poachers*; Psychrolutidae—fathead sculpins*; Bathylutichthyidae; Cyclopteridae—lump fish or lumpsuckers**; Liparidae—snailfish

\*THE AGONIDAE ARE DIVIDED INTO 4 SUBFAMILIES AND THE PSYCHROLUTIDAE INTO 2 (SEE ENTRY FOR SCULPINS AND POACHERS FOR FURTHER DETAILS)

\*\*THE CYCLOPTERIDAE ARE DIVIDED INTO 2 SUBFAMILIES (SEE ENTRY FOR LUMPSUCKERS AND SNAILFISH FOR FURTHER DETAILS)

→ **Somewhat reminiscent of a Japanese Samurai warrior, the spiny crown scorpionfish (Scorpaenopsis species) is also one of many venomous scorpionfish.**

The estuarine stonefish (*Synanceia horrida*) is often cited as the world's most venomous fish. One of its close, but less venomous, relatives (*Leptosynanceia asteroblepa*) can cause excruciating pain and kill a human in one to two hours. Equal to, or perhaps even surpassing, the estuarine stonefish in the strength of its venom is "the" stonefish (*S. verrucosa*). All three of these fish are members of the mail-cheeked fish (order Scorpaeniformes), a survey of which is presented in the following pages.)

Yet these poisonous fish are for the most part sedentary, and neither do they view humans as potential food. Instead, the reason they are sometimes responsible for injuries or even fatalities is because they are so hard to see. Because they look like rocks or weed-encrusted

objects on the seabed, it is very easy to step on one of these venomous creatures by mistake.

## Shared Stay

Not all mail-cheeked fish match the stonefish in terms of the strength of their venom. Many, though, like the lionfish, pack a powerful poisonous punch in the spines of their dorsal, pelvic, and pectoral fins. Many others are totally harmless despite carrying spines on their cheeks. The cheek spines, which are typical of most mail-cheeked fish, and which identify them as belonging to one large, though diverse, family group, arise from a bony structure usually referred to as a "stay" (or strut). This stay links the suborbital bones, located under the eye, with the "operculum" (gill cover). In some cases—for example, the lumpfish (family Cyclopteridae)—there is no spine on the suborbital stay, although the stay itself is still present.

In the case of the sablefish (two species that make up the family Anoplopomatidae) not only are there no spines on the suborbital stay, but pronounced differences

in body shape and structures, particularly the absolute lack of spines or ridges in the head, make them appear totally unrelated to the other members of the order. Indeed, that may turn out to be the case, but for the moment the fact that both species have the bony stay places them in the mail-cheeked fish order. Only time will tell whether or not the stay has in fact evolved quite independently in these fish.

## Diverse Group

Despite the shared characteristics of the suborbital stay, the order is made up of a hugely diverse group of fish, some of which match the image of a "scorpionfish" perfectly, while others look very little like one. In total, there are around 25 families, nearly 260 genera, and around 1,326 species (these numbers vary according to which classification is followed).

Among the most scorpionfishlike of the families are the members of the family Scorpaenidae, which include the lionfish, stonefish, waspfish, and the rockfish (the last depart a bit more than the others from the traditional image). Least scorpionfishlike, perhaps, are the orbicular velvetfish (family Caracanthidae), the helmet gurnards (family Dactylopteridae), the gurnards, or sea robins (family Triglidae), the various flatheads (families Bembridae, Platycephalidae, and Hoplicthyidae), the greenlings (family Hexagrammidae), the Baikal oilfish and allies (family Comephoridae), the snailfish (family Liparidae), and the sablefish and lumpfish.

## Egg-layers to Livebearers

In terms of breeding behavior most species lay eggs. There are, however, numerous species that depart from the classic egg-layer breeding style. In the rockfish (subfamily Sebastinae) the eggs are fertilized while they are still within the female's body. Once that has been achieved, these eggs are retained by the female for varying lengths of time depending on species. In some they are released right after fertilization, while in others they are retained not only until they hatch but for some time after. A similar procedure is found in the Baikal oilfish and some other types.

Therefore we find the full range of breeding strategies—from straightforward egg laying (oviparity) to livebearing (viviparity). The variations in this order have led to some dispute among scientists; some of their arguments are highlighted in the following pages.

Flying gurnard (*Dactylopterus volitans*)

**Common name** Gurnards

**Families** Dactylopteridae (flying and helmet gurnards), Triglidae (gurnards and sea robins)

**Subfamilies** Triglidae: Triglinae (gurnards and sea robins): Peristediinae (armored gurnards and armored sea robins)

**Order** Scorpaeniformes

**Number of species** Dactylopteridae: 7 in 2 genera; Triglidae: around 150 in 10 genera

**Size** From 2.8 in (7cm) to 35.4 in (90 cm)

**Key features** Elongated bodies, tapering toward tail; scutelike scales (helmet gurnards) or spine-covered plates (armored sea robins); head encased; eye ridges (gurnards), or helmetlike structure (flying and helmet gurnards); mouth located under tip of snout, either blunt (helmet gurnards), or 2 projections (gurnards and sea robins); barbels on underside of lower jaw (armored sea robins); two dorsal fins in all species; pectorals large and winglike (helmet gurnards) but smaller in others; several free rays in pectoral fin (gurnards); long spine in pelvic fins (helmet gurnards); varied coloration

**Breeding** Eggs and sperm released late spring or summer, then abandoned

**Diet** Bottom-dwelling invertebrates; some fish

**Habitat** Adults marine, juveniles may enter estuaries; helmet gurnards in tropical waters; mostly sandy bottoms; shallow water less than 655 ft (200 m) deep, some species over 2,950 ft (900 m)

**Distribution** Dactylopteridae: Atlantic and Indo-Pacific Oceans; Triglidae: widely distributed in most temperate and tropical seas: armored sea robins center on Atlantic, Indian, and Pacific Oceans

⬆ *The large rays of the pectoral fins of this 35.4-inch (90-cm) flying gurnard (Dactylopterus volitans) fan out over the sandy bottom as it searches for its favorite meal of crustaceans, especially crabs, clams, and small fish.*

# Gurnards

Dactylopteridae, Triglidae

*Not only can gurnards swim, but some can also "fly" through the water and "walk" along the bottom, using the rays of their pelvic or pectoral fins as wings, legs, or hands.*

IN ADDITION TO BEING AMONG the best walkers and underwater fliers of the fish world, the flying or helmet gurnards (family Dactylopteridae) are also among the best producers of sound. The other gurnard family (Triglidae), in the order Scorpaeniformes, is broken down into two subfamilies—Triglinae and Peristediinae.

## Noisy Talk

Helmet gurnards make sounds through "stridulation"—in other words, the rubbing together of some of the bones (hyomandibular bones) associated with the gill arches. The gurnards (family Triglidae) also produce sounds: in their case by vibrating the swim bladder.

Either way, gurnards are among the noisiest fish in the sea. They also produce more elaborate sounds than most, an honor they share with other noisy fish, such as the toadfish (family Batrachoididae) and the amazing drums (family Sciaenidae). They vibrate their body walls and amplify the sounds via their swim bladder.

The sounds produced by gurnards enable the fish to keep in touch with each other. Sounds can also be used in rivalry encounters between males, as well as in more amicable exchanges between males and females.

## Horns and Helmets

Related to the helmet gurnards, but not as closely as their names may suggest, are the gurnards, also known as the sea robins. This is a far larger family (Triglidae) containing over 150 species in two subfamilies. The gurnards, or sea robins, themselves form the subfamily Triglinae, with a total of some 113 species, while a distinctive group, usually referred to as

⟶ *The oriental flying gurnard (Dactyloptena orientalis) appears to have two large eyes on its pectoral fins, enough to disconcert a potential predator. The fish does not fly, as its name suggests, but gives that impression as it moves over the surface. It can also appear to walk by using the pelvic fins and pectoral fin rays.*

 **SEE ALSO** Toadfish **36**:54; Fish, Flying **38**:70; Snooks, Basses, Perches, and Drums **40**:12

# Underwater Flyers

The common name—flying gurnards—for the seven species that make up the family Dactylopteridae was originally given to these fish because it was thought that they could actually fly or glide through the air, much as the true flying fish do. However, as is so often the case, the real situation is quite different.

The large pectorals that these fish have are usually carried folded and close to the body. It is only when a flying gurnard is alarmed or feels threatened that it extends these winglike fins and flashes their bright colors, frequently scaring off a would-be predator.

At the same time, the gurnard takes off at speed with its "wings" held open. While it creates the impression of flying, the actual driving force is generated, as in the vast majority of fish, by the tail. Since we now know that flying gurnards do not fly, their original common name is gradually being replaced by the name "helmet gurnards" in view of their encased head.

the armored sea robins or armored gurnards, constitute the subfamly Peristediinae, containing about 40 species. In some of the most recent classifications the characteristics of the armored sea robins are regarded as sufficiently significant to warrant raising them to the level of a family.

The most obvious difference between these two types of gurnard and their "flying" cousins is the size of the pectoral fins, the members of

*⊕ The red gurnard (Aspitrigla cuculus) shows its bony head and blunt snout, and appears to be in the act of walking using its pectoral fins.*

the family Triglidae having shorter wings than the helmet gurnards. Some species, though, like the long-finned gurnard (*Lepidotrigla argus*), the northern sea robin (*Prionotus carolinus*), the striped sea robin (*P. evolans*), the latchet (*Pterygotrigla polyommata*), and others, have sizable pectoral fins. Nevertheless, they are modest when compared to those of the flying gurnard (*Dactylopterus volitans*) and its six closest relatives.

## Armored Sea Robins

In gurnards, or sea robins, and armored gurnards, or armored sea robins, the snout carries two projections, one on either side. They give the fish the appearance of having two horns, which are small in the gurnards but much larger in their armored cousins. The helmet gurnards do not have horns; instead, they have a large, blunt, bony, helmetlike head with spines and ridges. The body itself is covered in modified platelike scales (scutes), a feature that may be partly shared with both the gurnards and the armored gurnards.

The armored gurnards, for their part, can be easily distinguished from the two other groups by their barbels on the lower jaw. Some species can also be found in much deeper

water than their relatives. For example, the armored sea robin (*Peristedion miniatum*) from the western Atlantic, is a 12-inch (30-cm) species that can be found in waters as shallow as 210 feet (64 m) or as deep as 3,000 feet (910 m).

## Encased Food Fish

Gurnards of all three types have firm but tasty flesh; and although the size of the body may be relatively modest when compared to that of the head (particularly in the helmet gurnards), many species are fished commercially, although not on a large scale.

Among the helmet gurnards the most frequently fished species are the flying gurnard, the oriental flying gurnard (*Dactyloptena orientalis*), and the spotwing flying gurnard (*D. macracantha*), the last of which is frequently caught unintentionally in nets set out for other species. Because of their unusual pectoral fins the helmet gurnards are also popular exhibits in public aquariums.

## More Extensively Fished

Gurnards of the subfamily Triglinae are fished much more extensively and in larger quantities than those of the two other groups. Many species are, in fact, seen frequently in fish markets, where most are sold fresh; small quantities are also sold frozen.

The red-bodied streaked gurnard (*Chelidonichthys lastoviza*), which has an extensive eastern Atlantic range from Norway to the Cape of Good Hope and into the Indian Ocean toward Mozambique, is probably the most widely fished and marketed species; it is generally considered excellent eating, especially in Mediterranean countries. Also popular in these countries is the grayish tub, saphirine, or yellow gurnard (*C. lucerna*), one of the largest gurnards at around 30 inches (75 cm) long.

## Gurnard "Caviar"

Another member of this subfamily is the northern sea robin (*Prionotus carolinus*), ranging from Nova Scotia in Canada,

southward to the Gulf of Mexico. It is a beautifully finned species that is exploited in numerous ways—its eggs are sold as gurnard "caviar," its flesh is also sold as pet food or for bait, and its tissues are processed into fishmeal and fertilizer.

The armored gurnards, or sea robins, are the least exploited of the gurnards. Of the 40 or so species very few are ever seen in fish markets. The fact that most species are found in deep water—frequently below 1,640 feet (500 m)—is, undoubtedly, a significant factor.

But in addition, the spine-bearing plates that cover its slim body also make processing a less straightforward affair than it is in either the helmet gurnards or the "normal" gurnards. Locally, though, some species, like the African armored sea robin (*Peristedion cataphractum*), are targeted as food fish.

# Handwalkers and Footwalkers

While fish do not have arms and legs or, therefore, hands and feet, they do have structures that, in some ways, are equivalent. For example, the pectoral fins could be seen as representing the arms and hands of mammals, and the pelvic fins as legs and feet.

Applying this idea to helmet gurnards, gurnards, and armored gurnards, a significant difference between them becomes apparent. The helmet gurnards, for instance, have large pectoral fins that, while being winglike, do not have any free or separated rays (that is, rays not joined by a membrane). The bottom four rays are separated from the rest of the pectoral fin but function as a unit. In sharp contrast, the gurnards and their armored relatives have several free or separated rays in their pectoral fins that act independently of each other. Turning to the pelvic fins, the helmet gurnards have a long, powerful spine and several soft rays; the two other types lack this spine, having larger, softer pelvics instead.

Therefore the helmet gurnards choose to walk on their "feet," using their powerful pelvic spines to pace on the bottom by extending first one pelvic fin and then the other. Conversely, the gurnards and armored gurnards walk on their "hands," using the free rays of their pectoral fins to move on the seafloor. They also use these highly sensitive rays to detect buried food.

Ocean perch (*Sebastes marinus*)

**Common name** Scorpionfish, stonefish, and allies

**Family** Scorpaenidae

**Subfamilies** Sebastinae (rockfish), Scorpaeninae (scorpionfish), Sebastolobinae (thornyheads), Plectrogeninae, Pteroinae (lionfish, turkeyfish, dragonfish, or butterfly cods); Setarchinae, Neosebastinae (gurnard perches); Apistinae, Tetraroginae (waspfish or sailback scorpionfish), Minoinae (stingers), Choridactylinae (ghouls and relatives), Synanceinae (stonefish)

**Order** Scorpaeniformes

**Number of species** 380 in about 56 genera

**Size** From 1.6 in (4 cm) to 40 in (104 cm)

**Key features** Body elongated and tapering toward tail, usually compressed; head heavy and large with ridges and spines, especially on "cheeks"; eyes and mouth large; fins may carry elongated rays; dorsal, anal, and pelvic fins may have venomous spine glands; varied coloration

**Breeding** Mostly internal fertilization

**Diet** Invertebrates; also fish

**Habitat** Mainly marine; some enter brackish water; mainly shallow water, but some extend down to 6,560 ft (2,000 m)

**Distribution** All tropical and temperate seas

**Status** World Conservation Union lists: bocaccio (*Sebastes paucispinis*) as Critically Endangered because of overfishing; shortspine thornyhead (*Sebastolobus alascanus*) and acadian redfish (*Sebastes fasciatus*) as Endangered, also due to overfishing; Saint Helena deepwater scorpionfish (*Pontinus nigropunctatus*) as Vulnerable

⊕ *This 40-inch (100-cm) ocean perch (Sebastes marinus) is a popular food fish that is normally trawled in deep waters in the northern reaches on both sides of the Atlantic.*

# Scorpionfish, Stonefish, and Allies

Scorpaenidae

*The stonefish has a lethal disguise. It looks incredibly like a stone; but if someone wading in the sea unwittingly steps on one, the result could be fatal.*

TO ALL INTENTS AND PURPOSES these fish do not look like fish at all—if you can spot them, that is. Their rough, lump-ridden bodies are even covered in slimy algae (in some species), making them look more like stones than fish, hence their common name of stonefish.

## Poisoned Stones

The stonefish—family Scorpaenidae, subfamily Synanceinae, but classifications differ among some leading scientists—are widespread, mostly, but not exclusively, in tropical waters. Wherever they are found, they are feared, and with good reason, since they are probably the most poisonous fish in the world. Indeed, two species of stonefish—the estuarine stonefish (*Synanceia horrida*) and the stonefish (*S. verrucosa*)—are known to be the two most venomous fish on the planet.

In Australia the Queensland aboriginals even have a tribal dance whose aim is to teach

⊕ *The estuarine stonefish (Synanceia horrida) lives up to its name with its bizarre appearance. Cylindrical in shape and with close-set eyes, it waits patiently for its prey.*

58

the uninformed about the dangers posed by stonefish.

A wax model of a stonefish is buried inside a sacred area, and the elders dance around it until one of them "accidentally" steps on the model. The "mortally wounded" elder then brings proceedings to an abrupt end in a fit of agonized shrieks and convulsions.

In fact, this act is not far removed from the real thing, since victims of the stonefish sometimes die excruciatingly painful deaths within a short time of being stung.

Characteristically, stonefish have 13 venom-secreting spines along the ridge of their back. Spines on their anal and pelvic fins also carry venom.

There are between 10 and 12 species of stonefish (some classifications mention 34). Together these stonefish species form a distinct subgroup within a much larger group of venomous fish—the scorpionfish or rockfish.

## Killer Instinct or Self-defense?

The stonefish spends large parts of the day (and also the night) resting on the bottom, usually among rocks, but often partly buried in sandy patches between rocks, with their dorsal fin folded. They are camouflaged with a mottled pattern and, in some species, a thin covering of algae. Skin glands along the top of the body look like warts and give a knobby, irregular look to its surface.

The large mouth is held shut, apart from slight breathing movements, and is slanted upward at a sharp angle in all but two species—the pitted stonefish (*Erosa erosa*) and *Dampierosa daruna*. The eyes are located on the top of the skull and are directed outward and upward, apart from the two species mentioned above, in which they are directed outward.

When a suitable victim swims close enough to the mouth, the stonefish drops its lower jaw and, at the same time, lunges at its target. The

⬆ *The spectacular coloration of the red lionfish (Pterois volitans), native to the coral reefs of Micronesia, thinly disguises the venomous spines that deliver its poison.*

speed of these attacks is such that they can only be fully seen if filmed in slow motion.

When they are attacked, stonefish raise their fin spines in a reflex action, which can be fatal for humans if they touch or step on one. The fish is only acting in self-defense.

### Lions, Tigers, Dragons, Turkeys, and Butterflies

The lionfish (also called turkeyfish, tigerfish, dragonfish, scorpionfish, and butterfly cods) are spectacularly finned, colorful species that, like the stonefish, carry venom glands in their fin spines. Like most of the stonefish, they are tropical and also are members of the family Scorpaenidae. It is almost universally agreed that within the family lionfish form a distinct group of their own—the subfamily Pteroinae.

In total there are some 17 species distributed among five genera. The best known of them is, undoubtedly, *Pterois*, which contains some of the largest and most popular species in the marine aquarium hobby.

While stonefish rely on their camouflage and their spines for protection, and hunt by waiting for suitable prey to swim within lunging distance, lionfish often hunt in open water. When in hunting mode, these fish tend to spread their fins to their full extent and hover in the water, often with their head tilted slightly downward.

That makes them fully visible to their intended prey, although their overall shape, color shades and patterns, plus no obvious swimming movement also make them appear more like a clump of floating seaweed than a large-mouthed predator. Slowly, almost imperceptibly, they glide toward their target until they are close enough to launch their attack, which, as in the stonefish, consists of a high-speed lunge accompanied by a dropping of the lower jaw to create a strong sucking effect that drags the victim straight into the huge mouth.

These stealth hunters use an additional technique when going for prey close to coral

⬇ *The 4-inch (10-cm) sailfin waspfish (Paracentropogon species) has a compressed body and venomous spines. It is found in shallow coastal bays with sandy bottoms in the Indo-Pacific.*

heads or rockfaces. While still adopting the above strategy, they also use their pectoral fins to herd their prey into a corner, the large pectorals preventing any escape, before engulfing it in the typical ultrarapid gulp.

A third hunting technique used by at least some species is the sit-and-wait method. When adopting this approach, the lionfish chooses a ledge or mouth of a cave and uses its body colors and irregular overall shape to blend in with its surroundings. Here it can lie in wait, just as a stonefish does, until a suitable meal swims within range.

## Wide Distribution

The remaining 176 or so species of the lionfish's most closely related group belong to the 18 genera that feature most of the species that are commonly referred to as scorpionfish. Some are also called rockfish—for example, the offshore rockfish (*Pontinus kuhlii*)—or stingfish—for example, the weedy stingfish (*Scorpaenopsis cirrosa*).

Among this large subfamily, the Scorpaeninae, are some of the most widely distributed mail-cheeked fish, as well as some of the most fascinating. For example, two eastern-northern Atlantic species stretch all the way from the U.K. down to the Canary islands and into the Mediterranean and Black Sea. One such species—the large-scaled scorpionfish (*Scorpaena scrofa*), which grows to nearly 20 inches (50 cm) and weighs up to 6.6 pounds (3 kg)—is believed to extend even further. In fact, a very similar species that is found in South Africa is almost certainly a southerly component of the same population that occurs in the northernmost parts of the range.

The black scorpionfish (*S. porcus*) is a smaller species attaining nearly 15 inches (38 cm) in length and 2 pounds (0.9 kg) in weight. Although it can reach depths of 2,625 feet (800 m), it is still fished commercially, although not to the extent of its larger relative, which ranges from 65 to 1,640 feet (20–500 m).

Both these fish have delicate white, succulent flesh that is very highly rated,

## Hot Remedy

Stonefish and their close allies, the lionfish, turkeyfish, or butterfly cods, may not be overly aggressive, but their venomous defenses can cause excruciating pain and, in extreme cases, possibly death. Yet some lionfish are popular with aquarists despite the potential risk they pose.

However, few aquarists ever get stung, largely owing to the generally placid nature of lionfish, and even fewer people ever step on a stonefish. But when they do, prompt action can mean the difference between life and death. Most surprisingly, this remedy does not involve complicated or sophisticated medication. It is as simple, quite literally, as hot water.

The treatment works because heat breaks down (denatures) stonefish and lionfish venom (as well as other venoms). Therefore, if the affected part of the body is placed in water that is as hot as can be tolerated, and if the action is taken within minutes (before the venom has had a chance to spread throughout the body), the results (and cure) can be quite remarkable.

It is still necessary to seek medical assistance, though, particularly in the case of a stonefish sting. Antivenom medication is now available, at least in some of the regions, like Australia, where stonefish occur in places frequented by swimmers and divers.

particularly in Mediterranean countries, the Canaries, and Madeira, even though the bones are long and thin, and can be easily swallowed.

## From Leaves to Hairs to Decoys

The Scorpaeninae subfamily also contains the smallest scorpionfish of all—the diminutive pigmy scorpionfish (*Sebastapistes fowleri*), a reef-associated species from the Indo-Pacific that only grows to about 1.6 inches (4 cm). Yet, despite its apparently defenseless appearance, it has a potent venomous sting.

The leaf scorpionfish (*Taenionotus triacanthos*) has a huge dorsal fin. Although it has neither more spines or rays than other scorpionfish nor a larger base, its individual spines and rays are much longer than in many other species. Therefore, when the fin is extended, especially when the front spines are

tilted forward—in other words, extending over the head—the overall impression created is that of a leaf. This effect is further enhanced by the fish's movements, which consist of side-to-side swaying that mimics the movement of a leaf being rocked by gentle currents.

This widely distributed Indo-Pacific species is small at 4 inches (10 cm). It is unusual in that it changes (molts) its skin every two weeks or so, peeling from head to tail.

The hairy scorpionfish (*Scorpaenodes hirsutus*) is a shallow-water reef species also from the Indo-Pacific. It is small, at 2.4 inches (6 cm), and has tiny hairlike filaments all over its body that probably give it extra camouflage.

*⊙ Native to the western Pacific and Andaman Sea, the bearded ghoul (Inimicus didactylus) is normally buried in sand during daylight hours, with algae sometimes adding to the camouflage. It can put on a brilliant warning display with its pectoral fins if disturbed. This particular fish is an unusual red variant.*

## Pumped Venom

There are several reasons why stonefish venom is so effective. One is that it is a powerful neurotoxin—a poison that affects nervous tissue, at best damaging it, at worst killing it. In addition, there are grooves running along each spine along which the ducts of the poison glands run. Therefore, while the spines themselves are not poisonous, they hold the route by which the venom is injected.

When pressure is applied to these spines, for example, by stepping on a stonefish, it squeezes and activates the glands—in turn, resulting in drops of venom being pumped along the grooves and into the wounds created by the spines.

Lionfish lack spine grooves, and their venom is less potent than a stonefish's. Despite this, some deaths may also have occurred as a result of being stung by one of these *Pterois* species. Shown below are the venomous spines of a scorpionfish (*Scorpaenopsis* species).

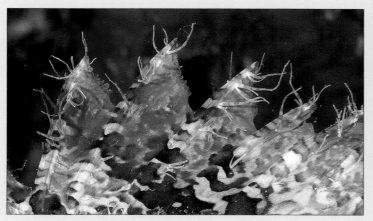

The most exceptional member of this family is probably the decoy scorpionfish (*Iracundus signifer*), although it must be said that the competition for this title is pretty intense. Like all its relatives in the subfamily, the decoy scorpionfish is a passive predator that blends in with its surroundings until a suitable meal swims within reach. However, the decoy scorpionfish also has a fishlike pattern on its dorsal fin, which it flashes repeatedly to lure a potential victim within reach.

## Long-lived Rockfish

While only a few members of the Scorpaeninae are known as rockfish, the exact opposite applies to the Sebastinae, in which the majority are referred to as rockfish. Some species are also known as rockcods, some as gurnard perches (see also Neosebastinae, below), others as sea or ocean perches, and several as redfish. A few have unique names such as the bocaccio (*Sebastes paucispinis*), the treefish (*S. serriceps*), and the chillipepper (*S. goodei*). In addition, a small group of seven species belonging to the subfamily

Sebastolobinae is generally referred to as the thornyheads.

In most traditional classifications these two subfamilies belong to the family Scorpaenidae, just as the lionfish and scorpionfish discussed in the preceding paragraphs do. In some of the most recent classifications (reflecting the differences of opinion that exist in the splitting of the mail-cheeked fish) the rockfish and thornyheads are regarded as members of a separate family, the Sebastidae, that has two subfamilies—Sebastinae and Sebastolobinae, respectively.

⊕ *The colors of this 4-inch (10-cm) leaf scorpionfish (*Taenianotus triacanthos*), from the Indo-Pacific, can vary from white and pink to red and green. It has a distinctive sail-like fin, a beardlike growth around its mouth, and a compressed body.*

Undeniably, some rockfish look a little more like perches overall than scorpionfish (though the similarity is superficial). Thornyheads are generally more similar to scorpionfish, however. Underlying the similarity of both these groups to the scorpionfish (and their distinct difference from perches) are the characteristic venomous spines that are found in most of the species.

Some rockfish are considered excellent food and game fish. Perhaps the most

outstanding is the slim-bodied, large-mouthed bocaccio, which grows to around 36 inches (90 cm) and weighs over 20 pounds (9.6 kg). It is neither the largest nor the heaviest of the rockfish, but it is one of the most active swimmers and hunters—hence its attraction to anglers. Longer and heavier and also popular as game fish are the cowcod (*Sebastes levis*), the yelloweye rockfish (*S. ruberrimus*), the quillback rockfish (*S. maliger*), and several others.

All these species have another feature in common, in that they are long-lived fish with estimated lifespans of over 50 years. In fact, the quillback is reported to live for 90 years. Yet even this species is relatively short-lived when compared to the rougheye rockfish (*S. aleutinus*), which has a lifespan of over 140 years, or the shortraker or silver-gray rockfish (*S. borealis*), which can live for 120 years.

## The "Other" Scorpionfish

In addition to the groups of scorpionfish already discussed, there are several other subfamilies (or families in certain classifications), making a total of approximately 380 that form the family Scorpaenidae (as defined by Nelson 1994).

Three of them consist of just a few species. For example, there are only two species within the single genus that constitutes the subfamily Plectrogeninae. Neither has a common name, and both are small. *Plectrogenium barsukovi* grows to around 2 inches (5 cm) and is found within a very narrow depth range of between 950 and 1,020 feet (290–310 m) on the Nasca Ridge in the southeastern Pacific. Like its slightly larger relative, *P. nanum*, which occurs at depths between 820 and 2,130 feet (250–680 m) in the Indo-Pacific, it has the typical venomous spines of most other members in the family.

With just three species the subfamily Apistinae represents the next smallest group of scorpionfish. They are found in much shallower water—around 195 feet (60 m) in the case of the ocellated waspfish (*Apistus carinatus*). Despite its small size of around 7 inches (18 cm), this Indo-West Pacific species is fished

commercially, but usually on a local basis, with small quantities sold either fresh, dried, or salted.

The subfamily Setarchinae contains five species, one of which—the midwater scorpionfish (*Ectreposebastes imus*)—is the scorpionfish that is best adapted for a free-swimming midwater existence. A widespread species found in the Atlantic, Indian, and Pacific Oceans, it measures about 7 inches (18 cm); it chases its prey, consisting largely of different types of shrimp, at depths ranging from around 490 feet (150 m) all the way down to 6,560 feet (2,000 m).

None of the members of the next subfamily (Minoinae), represented by 11 species of the genus *Minous* and generally referred to as stingfish, are midwater swimmers. Overall, they look very much like standard scorpionfish, except for one rather interesting difference. The lowermost ray of the pectoral fin is separated from the rest and carries a cap on its tip.

These small fish, the largest of which grow to around 6 inches (15 cm)—for example, the gray stingfish (*M. monodactylus*) from the Indo-West Pacific—are found on muddy and sandy bottoms, usually in shallow water, but can extend down to nearly 1,380 feet (420 m). It is believed that the extended capped pectoral fin ray helps them walk on these surfaces.

## The Gurnard Perches

Next in terms of numbers of species (12) is the subfamily Neosebastinae, commonly called the gurnard perches. The similarity to the gurnards (families Dactylopteridae and Triglidae), however, is very superficial. In fact, gurnard perches look more like scorpionfish than the rockfish mentioned above.

The main center of distribution of these bottom-dwelling species is Australia, where most species are found on rocky coastal reefs at depths ranging from very shallow water only a few feet deep down to a maximum depth of 850 feet (260 m) in the thetisfish (*Neosebastes thetidis*). Although some of the species—for example, the rough gurnard perch (*N. pandus*) —can grow to around 20 inches (50 cm), none is fished commercially.

The Choridactylinae, or Inimicinae, is a subfamily of 14 species in two genera: *Inimicus* and *Choridactylus*. Some are known as ghouls, while others (as in the subfamily Minoinae) are

*⊕ The 3-inch (7.6-cm) Ambon scorpionfish (Pteroidichthys amboinensis) occurs in the western Pacific. The appendages on its head make it look crablike or scorpionlike.*

# Internal Breeders

The rockfish and thornyheads (subfamilies Sebastinae and Plectrogeninae, respectively) employ internal fertilization. The eggs are fertilized inside the body of the female and are retained there for varying lengths of time.

In the shortspine thornyhead (*Sebastolobus alascanus*), for instance, the eggs are fertilized while still in the egg tube (oviduct) and are released into the water and abandoned shortly after. In the blackbelly rosefish (*Helicolenus dactylopterus dactylopterus*) the fertilized eggs are released into the water, but over a period of time. As a result, these eggs are at differing stages of development when they are ejected by the female.

In *Sebasticus marmoratus* (no common name) the fertilized eggs are retained inside the female until they hatch, at which point the female releases into the water larvae rather than eggs. The red gurnard perch (*Helicolenus percoides*) goes a stage further and holds on to the larvae until they are about 0.4 inches (1 cm) long before giving birth. A large female rockfish produces around 300,000 to 350,000 eggs—a considerable number, of course, but nowhere near the totals produced by some egg-laying species (several million in cod). This reduction in number is typical of species that employ internal fertilization, where the chances of each egg being fertilized are much higher than in species in which the eggs and sperm are scattered in open water.

called stingfish. While the Minoinae have a single separated ray of the pectoral fin, the ghouls and their closest relatives have two (in the *Inimicus* species) or three (in the *Choridactylus* species).

Like their relatives, they live on muddy or sandy bottoms and use these rays for creeping or walking along the soft sediments. Some, like the Chinese ghoul (*I. caledonicus*) and the deadly bearded ghoul (*I. didactylus*), are well camouflaged and easily missed.

Despite their venomous spines, several species are fished commercially, some on a minor scale, like the orange-banded stingfish (*Choridactylus multibarbus*)—or on a larger scale, as in *Inimicus japonicus*, which is cultured as a food fish in parts of its Japanese and East China Sea range. This species is also used in traditional Chinese medicine.

### Sailback Scorpionfish

The true waspfish, as distinct from the ocellated waspfish mentioned above, are also known as the sailback scorpionfish because of their impressive dorsal fin. There are around 40 species that together form the subfamily Tetraroginae.

Among them is the most unusual goblinfish (*Glyptauchen panduratus*), whose head is separated from the rest of the body by a distinct notch at the back of the skull that creates the impression of a neck.

Some species of Tetraroginae are fished for human consumption, but not in large quantities. Most, however, are of no commercial interest, although several are used in public aquarium displays, and at least three—the leaf goblinfish (*Vespicula depressifrons*), the bullrout (*Notesthes robusta*), and the cockatoo waspfish (*Ablatys taenionotus*)—occasionally are seen in home aquaria.

The waspfish also include the largest number of species of scorpionfish that venture either into brackish or even fresh water. Most notable of them is the bullrout (also called the kroki) from New South Wales in Australia and western New Guinea (Irian Jaya).

Spotted coral croucher (*Caracanthus maculatus*)

**Common name** Velvetfish

**Families** Caracanthidae (orbicular velvetfish or coral crouchers), Aploactinidae (velvetfish), Pataecidae (Australian prowfish), Gnathanacanthidae (red velvetfish), Congiopodidae (pigfish, horsefish, or racehorses)

**Order** Scorpaeniformes

**Number of species** Caracanthidae: 5 in 1 genus; Aploactinidae: nearly 40 in about 17 genera; Pataecidae: about 5 in 3 genera; Gnathanacanthidae: 1 in 1 genus; Congiopodidae: 9 in 4 genera

**Size** From 0.35 in (0.9 cm) to 30 in (76 cm)

**Key features** Circular or elongated body; head shape variable; mouth frequently directed upward; sometimes spines on cheeks or head; dorsal fin notched or continuous; pelvic fins absent or very small; body scaleless or fully scaled; coloration: bright spots on plain background (orbicular velvetfish); mottled patterning in many velvetfish and pigfish; red blotches and radiating eye streaks on plain background in red velvetfish

**Breeding** No details available

**Diet** Wide variety of invertebrates

**Habitat** Tropical, subtropical, or temperate, even subantarctic (pigfish); all primarily bottom-dwellers: orbicular velvetfish closely associated with branched corals; velvetfish also found over muddy, sandy, or rocky bottoms

**Distribution** Caracanthidae and Aploactinidae: mainly Indian and Pacific Oceans; other three families: Southern Hemisphere, mainly around Australia, including Tasmania

⊕ *The 2-inch (5-cm) spotted coral croucher (Caracanthus maculatus) inhabits crests of shallow coral reefs, with a depth range of between 10 and 50 feet (3–15 m). It occurs from the East Indies north to Japan and through Micronesia.*

# Velvetfish

Caracanthidae, Aploactinidae, Pataecidae, Gnathanacanthidae, Congiopodidae

*The four tiny but beautiful representatives of the reef-associated family Caracanthidae are almost spherical and velvety-smooth to the touch, hence their common name of "orbicular velvetfish."*

ORBICULAR VELVETFISH ARE "SMOOTH AS VELVET" because they are scaleless but are covered in a thin layer of body mucus. To be more precise, while the body is scaleless, there are some tiny scales on top of the head, as well as below the base of the dorsal fin, but they do not affect the overall velvety look and feel of these fish.

## Coral Hunters

Orbicular velvetfish, or coral crouchers (family Caracanthidae), spend their lives swimming, hiding, and hunting for small creatures between the branches of species of branched corals like *Acropora*, *Pocillopora*, and *Stylophora*. The spaces between these branches are often very narrow, but they are negotiated easily by these velvetfish, which are both small and highly compressed (that is, flattened from side to side).

Three of the four species—the spotted croucher (*Caracanthus madagascariensis*), the spotted coral croucher (*C. maculatus*), and the pygmy coral croucher (*C. unipinna*)—are known to grow to around 2 inches (5 cm) in length. The fourth species, *C. typicus*, from Hawaii is little known, but it is thought that it grows no larger than 2.8 inches (7 cm).

## Prickly Velvetfish

Closely related to the orbicular velvetfish are the velvetfish, a family (Aploactinidae) of nearly 40 species. Whereas the velvety feel that the coral crouchers have is produced by their scaleless bodies, the smoothness in these fish is produced, surprisingly, by its scales.

In fact, the body of most velvetfish is completely covered in scales, but (and this is the crucial factor) they are modified into tiny

⊕ *The spotted coral croucher (Caracanthus maculatus) has a laterally compressed body and grows to no more than 2 inches (5 cm) long. Its unique texture, created by a body mucus, is enhanced by the spotted coloring.*

prickles that, being very close together, create the velvety appearance, as is the case with most species. Some are smooth due to a lack of scales. Two species that fall into this category are *Eschemeyer nexus*, a 1.8-inch (4.5-cm) species from Fiji, and *Matsubarichthys inusitatus*, which is known from just one specimen collected off Queensland in Australia (see box "Unique Specimen").

## Modified Scales

Other species have differently modified scales than the ones that create the velvetlike characteristic, and they, quite naturally, feel different. In *Xenaploactis cautes* from the western Pacific, for instance, the prickles are more like true spines. The threefin velvetfish (*Neoaploactis tridorsalis*) is also from the western Pacific. It is so called not because it really has

⊕ *Weber's velvetfish (Paraploactis obbesi) is a tropical species found in the Western Pacific. Like all seven species of the genus it is bottom dwelling around coastlines.*

three dorsal fins, but because the front few spines of the dorsal fin are separated from the rest, while a notch further back completes the appearance of three separate fins. The spiny scales are expanded at the tips so that they form a bladelike structure.

In terms of spectacular dorsal fins no velvetfish can surpass the crested scorpionfish (*Ptarmus jubatus*) from the western Indian Ocean. When this fish raises its dorsal fin, it tilts the first few spines forward at an angle; while the remaining spines follow in a fan shape, they become progressively larger, then smaller. Since the front of the fin lies above the eyes and the back lies close to the tail, the overall effect created is that of an impressive crest.

Velvetfish are shallow-water species often associated with coral reefs, also occurring over muddy, sandy, or rocky bottoms. Most measure less than 4 inches (10 cm), but a few are larger; the largest is *Aploactisoma milesii*, around 9 inches (23 cm), from Australian and Tasmanian waters. While all the species have spines, they rarely, if ever, cause painful injuries.

### Prowfish from Down Under

Impressive though the crested scorpionfish is in terms of dorsal fin development, it is surpassed by five species from Australian waters that have truly magnificent dorsals. They are the prowfish of the family Pataecidae, the largest of which grows to around 12 inches (30 cm).

Like the orbicular velvetfish, prowfish are scaleless and therefore smooth to the touch. However, they lack pelvic fins, and the dorsal fin extends from just in front of the eyes all the way to the tail, which it may join, as in the red indianfish (*Pataecus fronto*).

This species is also the most impressive of the prowfish, especially when it extends its

## Unique Specimen

The "holotype" of *Matsubarichthys inusitatus*—in other words, the specimen on which the species description was based—had an extremely large head for its body length. However, since it only measured 0.35 inches (0.9 cm) from its snout to the base of its caudal fin (for a definition of "Standard Length" see Glossary), the term "large" is relative. This species may well be the smallest velvetfish and the smallest mail-cheeked fish; but since we know next to nothing about it, it would be unwise to jump to conclusions on the basis of just one specimen.

Although *Matsubarichthys* has a scaleless body, it is not totally scaleless. It has a row of scales along the lateral line organ. These scales are unusual in that they are reported as being "extremely long and tubular," always bearing in mind that nothing can be extremely long in a 0.35 inch fish!

dorsal fin fully to give an excellent impression of a prow.

Prowfish are generally between 8 and 12 inches (20-30 cm) long, but one species, the whiskered prowfish (*Neoptataecus waterhousii*) from South Australian waters, grows to just 2.4 inches (6 cm). Like its closest relatives, it is a bottom-dweller from shallow to relatively shallow waters. The red indianfish, whose depth range is better known, is found at depths of between 130 and 260 feet (40–80 m).

## The One and Only Red Velvetfish

The Gnathanacanthidae is the smallest of the velvetfish families. It is "monotypic"; that is, it has only one genus and species—the red velvetfish (*Gnathanacanthus goetzeei*). Like some prowfish, the red velvetfish is a temperate species; it is also, like them and the orbicular velvetfish, or coral crouchers, scaleless. Unlike prowfish, *G. goetzeei* has well-formed pelvics.

It is a 12-inch (30-cm) shallow-water species that tends to be found in caves, under ledges, or in other forms of shelter in western and south Australian waters. The red part of its name refers to the reddish (more deep orange than bright red), roundish, and elongated patches that it carries on its plain-colored body. Streaks that radiate out from the eye give this unusual fish a very distinctive look. So do the

⊕ *The warty prowfish (Aetapcus maculatus), which is found in the shallow coastal waters off southern Australia, uses a unique defense system, expelling a venomous cloud from a vent near the gills.*

two dorsal fins, the first of which is crestlike and smaller than the back one.

## Pigs and Racehorses

As with many velvetfish, pigfish are scaleless. Some have smooth skin and are therefore velvety, while others have a granular surface.

All are bottom-dwellers from subtropical, temperate, or even cooler waters of the Southern Hemisphere. For example, the spiny horsefish (*Zanclorhynchus spinifer*) is found at depths between 16 and 1,310 feet (5–400 m) in the cold waters of the Southern Ocean.

This horsefish is a rather elongate, very spiny fish (hence its name) that grows to about 15.7 inches (40 cm) and feeds on bottom-living invertebrates. It is fished commercially, though not in large quantities.

In this particular species the spiny front part of the dorsal fin begins further back on the body than in most of the other species. These others tend to look a little like some of the velvetfish of the family Aploactinidae discussed earlier in this entry, while the spiny horsefish looks more like a long-snouted scorpionfish of the family Scorpaenidae covered in the previous entry.

## The Most Unusual Pigfish

Two species of pigfish are fished occasionally in even smaller quantities than the spiny horsefish—the smooth horsefish (*Congiopodus torvus*), the largest member of the family at around 30 inches (76 cm), and—the most unusual pigfish of them all—the spinenose horsefish (*C. spinifer*), which grows to nearly 18 inches (45 cm). It is not an unusual fish in terms of its shape, but because it sheds its outer flaky, fibrous, hardish layer of skin from time to time.

The pigfish family is probably the least known of the scorpionfish (suborder Scorpaenoidei), probably because of the distribution of the species and their deepwater habits. *Congiopodus kieneri* from Peruvian and Chilean waters and the spinenose horsefish, for example, can both be found at depths of around 1,640 feet (500 m).

**Fringelip flathead (*Eurycephalus otaitensis*)**

**Common name** Flatheads

**Families** Bembridae (deepwater flatheads), Platycephalidae (flatheads), Hoplichthyidae (ghost flatheads)

**Order** Scorpaeniformes

**Number of species** Bembridae: 8 in 3 genera; Platycephalidae: about 66 in 18 genera; Hoplichthyidae: 10 or 11 in 1 genus

**Size** From 2.8 in to 4 ft (1.2 m)

**Key features** Elongated bodies and flattened heads: least flattened in deepwater flatheads, most flattened in ghost flatheads; pointed snout with large mouth at tip directed upward; body scaleless in ghost flatheads but with line of scutes running length of body; 2 dorsal fins, front spiny and shorter than back; well-formed pectoral and pelvic fins; coloration: reddish in most deepwater flatheads, mottled in most others

**Breeding** Eggs and sperm scattered into water; eggs take about 1 day to hatch; larvae are planktonic; dusky flathead may be protrandrous hermaphrodite (juveniles are male then female)

**Diet** Invertebrates and smaller fish

**Habitat** Deepwater flatheads and ghost flatheads marine; flatheads predominantly marine; most found over sandy or muddy bottoms, sometimes associated with reefs or rocky terrains; some occur in deep to very deep water down to a depth of 4,920 ft (1,500 m)

**Distribution** Indo-Pacific

⬆ *The 12-inch (30-cm) fringelip flathead (*Eurycephalus otaitensis*) buries itself in the sand of lagoon and seaward reefs for camouflage—helped by its mottled pattern and many spines—to wait for a meal of crab and prawns.*

# Flatheads

Bembridae, Platycephalidae, Hoplichthyidae

*All flatheads have a relaxed "sit-and-wait" predatory style. They are well-camouflaged bottom-dwellers that bury themselves in the sand, lying in wait for their next meal.*

LIVING ON SANDY OR MUDDY bottoms, the well-camouflaged giant crocodilefish (*Cymbacephalus beauforti*) and the crocodile flathead (*Cociella crocodila*) lie in wait for their prey, usually small fish and crustaceans. They are two of about 66 species, together with the bartail flathead (*Platycephalus indicus*), that make up the family known as the flatheads (Platycephalidae). Along with another 10 to 11 species—the ghost flatheads (family Hoplichthyidae) and 8 species of deepwater flatfish (family Bembridae)—these fish form a distinctive group of scorpionlike or mail-cheeked fish that are grouped in their own suborder: the Platycephaloidei.

## Flat-headed Bottom-dwellers

Their main shared characteristics are that they are all elongated fish with flat heads, usually adorned with ridges and spines—as in most of the other groups belonging to the mail-cheeked fish in the order Scorpaeniformes. They also have two separate dorsal fins, a feature shared with fish like gurnards or sea robins, the red velvetfish, and other members of the order.

Flatheads are predominantly marine fish, though some are also found in brackish waters, and young bartail flatheads are even seen in fresh water. While many species are found in shallow or relatively shallow water, some (most notably among ghost, but not deepwater, flatheads), can be found at considerable depths down to below 4,920 feet (1,500 m). All are passive predators that use their camouflage to make themselves virtually invisible.

➡ *The giant crocodilefish (*Cymbacephalus beauforti*) is a member of the family Platycephalidae. It gets its name from its large, crocodile-shaped mouth.*

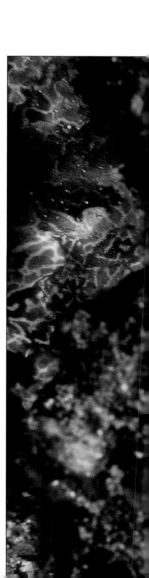

### Exotic Native

The main center of distribution for the bartail flathead (*Platycephalus indicus*) is the Indo-West Pacific. However, it was introduced along the Mediterranean coasts of both Israel (from the nearby Red Sea in 1945) and Egypt (in 1961).

The bartail flathead is now established in these regions to such an extent that few people are aware that it is not a native species. It has now made its home in its adopted Egyptian and Israeli waters, where it is regarded as an important game and food fish. It is also cultured for the food market in Japan.

### Fishing for Flatheads

The deepwater flatheads (family Bembridae) are found in water between 490 feet (150 m) and 2,130 feet (650 m) deep. There are currently eight species in the family, characterized by a cylindrical body and flat head. Maximum size is attained by *Bembras japonica* from the Indo-West Pacific, which grows to around 12 inches (30 cm). None of the deepwater flatheads are fished commercially.

However, some of the flatheads (family Platycephalidae) are fished in significant quantities, partly because they occur in shallow waters, and partly because some of the species grow larger than their deepwater flathead cousins. The dusky flathead (*Platycephalus fuscus*), a species that is endemic to Australia, grows to nearly 4 feet (1.2 m) and weighs around 33 lb (15 kg).

The ghost flatheads (family Hoplichthyidae) have the flattest, broadest heads of all; they also lack scales, though they have a row of scutes running from head to tail. The armored flathead (*Hoplichthis haswelli*) is the largest species. It is a southwest Pacific fish that grows to about 17 inches (43 cm) and is found on the continental shelf and slope at depths of 460 to 2,300 feet (140–700 m). Yet, despite this depth range, it is the only species of ghost flathead that is fished commercially to any extent.

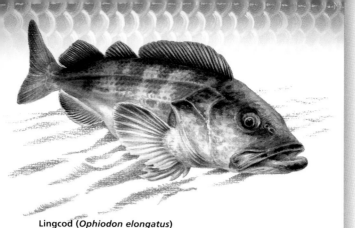

Lingcod (*Ophiodon elongatus*)

**Common name** Greenlings

**Family** Hexagrammidae

**Subfamilies** Hexagramminae (greenlings), Pleurogramminae (Atka mackerel), Ophiodontinae (lingcod), Oxylebinae (painted greenling), Zaniolepidinae (combfish)

**Order** Scorpaeniformes

**Number of species** 12 in 5 genera

**Size** From 10 in (25 cm) to 5 ft (1.5 m)

**Key features** Elongated bodies; head with pointed snout rounded at tip; mouth relatively large; lingcod has large, fanglike teeth separated by smaller teeth; head with cirri; dorsal fin with long base and notch separating front (spinous) part from back (soft-rayed) portion; notch particularly pronounced in combfish, anal fin also long-based; first 2 pelvic fin rays thickened in combfish; coloration: generally mottled and relatively subdued

**Breeding** Female releases masses of eggs deposited in cracks, on gravel, under rocks or ledges, and guarded by male; may take up to 8 to 10 weeks to hatch; larvae are planktonic for a time

**Diet** Invertebrates, particularly crustaceans and worms; also sea urchins and fish

**Habitat** Mainly rocky and sandy areas, often with seaweed such as kelp; shallow (even shoreline) or relatively shallow waters; some species extend to great depths, to nearly 1,900 ft (580 m)

**Distribution** Northern Pacific Ocean ranging from Alaska southward to Baja California, Mexico

⊕ *This 60-inch (1.5-m) lingcod (Ophiodon elongatus) has small, pointed teeth interspersed with large, fanglike teeth. Adults feed on crustaceans, octopuses, and squid, the young on copepods.*

# Greenlings

Hexagrammidae

*Most greenlings are known primarily as important food and game fish, popular with sporting anglers and commercial fisheries alike.*

THE LINGCOD (*OPHIODON ELONGATUS*), AN ELONGATED, bottom-dwelling fish, occurs along the western coast of the U.S. all the way from the Gulf of Alaska down to Baja California in Mexico. It can be found in shallow water (often close to rocks) or water as deep as 1,560 feet (475 m). It is a large, meaty fish with a length of nearly 5 feet (1.5 m) and weighing some 130 pounds (59 kg). It has excellent flesh and is therefore fished commercially. It is also a prize catch for anglers and has become a top game fish along the Pacific Coast of the U.S.

## Pacific Breeder

Since its north-south distribution is so extensive, the breeding season varies according to geographical location. Off the coast of British Columbia, for example, spawning can occur between February and April. A little farther south, off the Washington coast, it can begin in December and possibly extend into June, while off the California coast it can span the period between November and March. Large numbers of eggs are laid in crevices or under rocks in a mass that can weigh as much as 15 pounds (6.8 kg) and take between 8 and 10 weeks to hatch. The male guards them during this time.

## Valuable Food and Sport Fish

The ling is a member of the cod family; so is the cod (obviously). The lingcod is neither a ling nor a cod but looks a little like both of them. It is one of those numerous cases among fish in which the common name "points" in one direction, while the real identity of the species lies in a totally different one. In this case the differences are very large, while the similarities are, at best, extremely superficial.

The lingcod is a member of the small family of greenlings (Hexagrammidae) that consists of

⊕ *The rock greenling (Hexagrammos lagocephalus) is altogether brighter in coloration than the painted greenling and even has a bright blue color to the inside of its mouth, the last thing its prey is likely to see.*

just 12 species. Except for three species, all the rest are considered either important food fish, game fish, or both. In fact, one—*Hexagrammos otakii* (no English-language name)—mainly from Japanese and southern Korean waters, is deemed a sufficiently important food fish in Japan for it to be cultured for this purpose.

Perhaps even more important in terms of quantities fished is the Okhostk Atka mackerel (*Pleurogrammus azonus*). This species can grow to around 24 inches (60 cm) in length and gathers in large shoals near the surface during its juvenile phase.

As in other members of the family, the spawning season for these species spans the fall to winter months. Also, as in the lingcod, the female releases the eggs as a mass that she deposits in cracks, gravel, or among rocks. The male stands guard until they hatch.

Although greenlings can extend to considerable depths—down to nearly 1,900 feet (575 m) in the case of the Atka mackerel (*Pleurogrammus monopterygius*)—most are caught in either shallow or relatively shallow water. They are usually found over rocky and sandy bottoms or among seaweeds, such as kelp. In fact, one species is so closely associated with kelp that it is actually called the kelp greenling (*Hexagrammos decagrammus*).

## Three of a Kind

In addition to the lingcod and the other eight food and game fish members of the family there are three species that form a subgroup of their own—the painted greenling (*Oxylebius pictus*), the shortspine combfish (*Zaniolepis frenata*), and the longspine combfish (*Z. latipinnis*), which is the largest at around 12 inches (30 cm).

The most distinctive feature is that the notch on the dorsal fin (which all species have) is set much nearer the tail and is particularly deep in the combfish. The first three spines are also longer. In addition, there are other fin and body differences that have led a growing number of scientists to the conclusion that these three species belong in a family of their own named the combfish (the family Zaniolepidae). None of these species is regarded either as a food fish or a game fish, although the painted greenling—also known as the convict fish because of the stripes on its body— is sometimes hooked by anglers aiming for other target species.

Bullhead (*Cottus gobio*)

**Common name** Sculpins, poachers, and allies

**Families** Cottidae (sculpins), Cottocomephridae (Baikal sculpins), Comephoridae (Baikal oilfish), Abyssocottidae (deep-sea sculpins), Rhamphocottidae (grunt sculpin), Ereuniidae (ereunids), Psychrolutidae (fatheads), Agonidae (poachers), Hemitripteridae (hemitripterids), Bathylutichthyidae (bathyluctids)

**Order** Scorpaeniformes

**Number of species** Cottidae: about 200 to 300 in around 70 genera; Cottocomephridae: 7 in 3 genera; Comephoridae: 2 in 1 genus; Abyssocottidae: about 23 in 6 genera; Rhamphocottidae: 1 in 1 genus; Ereuniidae: 3 in 2 genera; Psychrolutidae: 40 in 10 genera; Agonidae: 46 in about 17 genera; Hemitripteridae: 9 in 3 genera; Bathylutichthyidae: 1 in 1 genus

**Size** From 0.8 in (2 cm) to 39 in (99 cm)

**Key features** Slim, elongated bodies (poachers) or robust (flatheads); head long and pointed (poachers), large and less pointed (Baikal oilfish), or blunt (miller's thumb and fatheads); mouth often large; usually 2 dorsal fins, anterior spiny and posterior soft-rayed, but only single dorsal fin (some poachers); dorsal, caudal, and anal joined (Bathylutichthyidae); pectoral fins well formed in most species; pectorals have several free rays (Ereuniidae); varied coloration

**Breeding** Eggs usually laid on roof of cave and guarded by male; most fertilization external

**Diet** Fish eggs, numerous invertebrates, and other fish

**Habitat** Fresh waters in streams, rivers, and lakes, to deep polar waters

**Distribution** Most seas, including polar regions; predominantly Northern Hemisphere

**Status** World Conservation Union lists 9 species of Cottidae family as: 2 Data Deficient, 4 Vulnerable, 2 Critically Endangered, 1 Extinct

⊕ *Bullheads (Cottus gobio) grow up to 7 inches (18 cm). They feed on bottom-dwelling invertebrates, insects, and crustaceans.*

# Sculpins, Poachers, and Allies

Cottidae, Cottocomephridae, Comephoridae, Abyssocottidae, Rhamphocottidae, Ereuniidae, Psychrolutidae, Agonidae, Hemitripteridae, Bathylutichthyidae

*The miller's thumb was one of the two sculpin species regularly caught by European children in previous centuries. They were usually found during pond- and stream-dipping expeditions.*

THE MILLER'S THUMB (*COTTUS GOBIO*) is reported as growing to around 7 inches (18cm) and having a lifespan of about five years. The vast majority of male specimens, though (males are larger than females), are usually a little over half this size. It is a predominantly freshwater species that occurs widely over most of Europe in streams, rivers, and lakes with a stony bottom.

## Dwarves and Giants

The cabezón (*Scorpaenichthys marmoratus*), from the northeastern Pacific, looks a bit like a giant version of the miller's thumb or bullhead (cabezón means "large head"), but it is quite different. For a start, it is strictly marine, occurring at depths ranging from the surface down to around 655 feet (200 m). It grows to a maximum length of 39 inches (99 cm) and can weigh as much as 30 pounds (14 kg). Quite unlike the miller's thumb, it is a species that is both fished commercially and regarded as a game fish. The flesh of the cabezón is deemed very good, but its eggs are poisonous.

Both the miller's thumb and the cabezón are members of the sculpin family (Cottidae), containing around 300 species. While the cabezón is the largest member of the family, other species can also be quite substantial. For example, the shorthorn sculpin (*Myoxocephalus scorpius*), which occurs on both sides of the Atlantic (generally in the more northern parts), as well as the Arctic, can attain a length of around 35.4 inches (90 cm),

⊕ *The miller's thumb (Cottus gobio), also known as a bullhead, normally frequents fast-flowing, shallow waters. Spiny dorsal and pectoral fins project from each side of the body of this specimen, which is resting on a stony streambed.*

but it is not fished commercially or sought out by anglers.

At the other end of the size spectrum are tiny species, such as *Daruma sagamia* and *Atopocottus tribranchius* (no English-language common names), both from Japanese waters. These dwarfs of the sculpin family measure only a little over 1.2 inches (3 cm).

### Baikal Sculpins

Baikal Lake is a long, narrow freshwater lake in Siberia. With a maximum depth of 5,315 feet (1,620 m) it is also the deepest lake in the world; its average depth is nearly 2,400 feet (730 m). It is about 395 miles (636 km) long and an average of 30 miles (48 km) wide, and contains about one-fifth of all the world's surface fresh water.

It is also home to 56 species of fish, and no fewer than 32 sculpins belonging to three separate families. Of these, 29 species are endemic to the lake (found nowhere else).

Some 23 species out of the 32 are known as deep-sea sculpins (family Abyssocottidae), a strange designation since Baikal Lake does not contain sea water, although it can be regarded as an inland sea.

The deep-sea sculpins are long, slim fish with pointed heads and predatory instincts. None is larger than 11 inches (29 cm), the largest being the red sculpin (*Procottus jeittelesii*). The smallest may be the dwarf sculpin (*P. gurwicii*) at around 2.4 inches (6.2 cm); since only one specimen has ever been recorded, we do not know if it is the maximum size for the species.

Although the only dwarf sculpin male was collected no deeper than 305 feet (93 m), deep-sea sculpins do not generally occur any shallower than about 560 feet (175 m). Some, in fact, are real deepwater specialists that fit their name perfectly. *Neocottus werestschagini* and *Asprocottus abyssalis* (no common names) can be found as deep as 4,595 feet (1,400 m). And the short-headed sculpin (*Cottinella boulengeri*) goes

*The Pacific staghorn sculpin (Leptocottus armatus) is found in bays and estuaries where it feeds on crabs and shrimp in the sand or, as in this case in Barkley Sound, Canada, herring roe. It is capable of producing a low-pitched noise when in danger.*

## Sculpins in Danger

Considering the fact sculpins are so widespread and occupy such diverse habitats, it is perhaps a little surprising that only nine species are listed officially by the World Conservation Union as facing threats to their survival.

Of these, two are listed as Data Deficient. The slender sculpin (*Cottus tenuis*) and the Klamath Lake sculpin (*C. princeps*) are both North American species from the Klamath River region in Oregon. No decision has been arrived at regarding the threats they face, but both are known to be uncommon, and the latter is no longer present in one of the key parts of its range, the Lost River.

Moving up the risk ladder, the rough sculpin (*C. asperrimus*), the Bear Lake sculpin (*C. extensus*), the Shoshone sculpin (*C. greenei*), and the Wood River sculpin (*C. leiopomus*) are all listed as Vulnerable. All of them have very restricted North American distributions that immediately put their future in doubt. Some, like the rough sculpin, are still common, but their range is extremely small, while others, like the Shoshone sculpin, are both restricted and uncommon.

The pygmy sculpin (*C. paulus*) is found only in Coldwater Springs, part of the Coosa River system, in Calhoun County, Alabama. It is not just extremely restricted but also rare. It is, therefore, now protected as a Critically Endangered species.

The worst case of all is the Utah Lake sculpin (*C. echinatus*), which was once relatively abundant in Utah Lake but is now presumed to be extinct.

even deeper—down to 5,250 feet (1,600m), as does *Abyssocottus gibbosus* (no common name). Yet, for all their deepwater resistance, all are small species, ranging between 3.9 and 5.5 inches (9.8–14 cm) in length.

At the other end of the depth range are the seven species that make up the family Cottocomephoridae (or subfamily Cottocomephorinae depending on which classification is followed). They are mostly "coastal" species found relatively close to the shores of the lake. Nevertheless, some of the species can be found both in shallow and relatively deep waters. For example, the flat sculpin (*Batrachocottus nikolskii*) is equally at home either at 13 feet (4 m) or at 1,560 feet (476 m), while *B. multiradiatus* (no common name) extends all the way from 164 feet (50 m) down to 2,625 feet (800 m).

The sculpins belonging to this family (or subfamily) have blunter snouts than their "deep-sea" relatives. They also have beautiful large pectoral fins that look almost like butterfly wings. Like the deep-sea sculpins, the flat sculpin and its relatives are hunters that feed, mostly, on invertebates.

Most remarkable of all the Baikal Lake sculpins are the two species of *Comephorus*, called oilfish owing to their high fat content that gives them a translucent appearance, which is emphasized by the scaleless body.

These slim-bodied, large-headed, large-mouthed sculpins also have porous bones that make them exceptionally light. As a result of this combination of little weight and high fat content, Baikal oilfish float to the surface when they die, often remaining trapped in ice till the spring of the following year, when they are washed up on the lakeshore.

However, it is their breeding behavior that really sets them apart. While other sculpins are

# Caveman Tactics

The miller's thumb is a species in which the males become intensely territorial during the breeding season. The male will find himself a large, flattish stone and create a shallow depression underneath it. It will become his spawning cave that he will defend against all comers. Depending on how severe he considers a threat, he will open his mouth, flare his gills and large pectoral fins, shake his head, or even croak or grunt before resorting to an attack.

He will also use these techniques whenever a female approaches. If she is not ready for spawning, she will take the hint and make a quick escape. However, if she is ripe with eggs, she will not swim away, and the male will entice her into his cave. He may even resort to grabbing her by the head and dragging her in.

The pink to yellow eggs, numbering between 100 and 500, are laid on the roof of the cave where they are fertilized by the male. The female then plays no further part and will be chased off by the male if she lingers. Subsequently the male will try to attract further females to his spawning cave and will guard the eggs until they hatch some three weeks later. However, he will not protect the larvae once they hatch—he may even eat them!

typical egg-layers in which eggs and sperm are released into the water where fertilization takes place, in the Baikal oilfish up to 3,000 eggs are fertilized while still inside the female's body. She then retains them until they hatch. These species are the only sculpin livebearers.

In the case of the smaller of the species, the little Baikal oilfish (*Comephorus dybowskii*) —but possibly also in the big Baikal oilfish (*C. baikalensis*)—it appears that most females die after releasing their young. Some, though, may survive for a second spawning, and even fewer may produce a third brood (see box).

### The Other Sculpins

There are about 90 other species that are generally referred to as sculpins and distributed over five families.

The grunt sculpin (*Rhamphocottus richardsoni*) has its own family all to itself—the Rhamphocottidae. It is a small 3.3-inch (8.3-cm) species from the northern half of the Pacific. It is found in tidal pools and rocky bottoms down to around 540 feet (165 m) and can use its

The pogge (Agonus cataphractus) *displays barbels under the head. It has eight rows of spines running along the body from head to tail, and it also has spines that protrude from the snout.*

pectoral fins to crawl over rocks or from one pool to another. It also has very interesting breeding behavior in that the female corners a male in a rock crevice or cave and will not allow him to leave until she lays her eggs and he fertilizes them.

The three members of the family Ereuniidae are not well known. They are deepwater species, mainly from around Japan, extending down to 1,870 feet (575 m). These fish, at a maximum size of around 12 inches (30 cm), look a little like gurnards (family Triglidae)—with a high, pointed head, slim, tapering body, and several free rays in the pectoral fins with which they can walk along the bottom. One example is *Marukawichthys ambulator*.

## Fatheads and Poachers

The fatheads (family Psychrolutidae) are much more numerous (about 40 species) and characterized, as befits their name, by a large, bulky head. As in some other families, several species are found in deep water. For example, the blotch-bodied polar sculpin (*Cottunculus microps*) from the more northern regions of the Atlantic can occur anywhere from around 560 feet (170 m) down to 3,280 feet (1,000 m). Impressive though their depth range may be, it

is modest when compared with the blob sculpin (*Psychrolutes phrictus*) from the North Pacific. At 27.5 inches (70 cm) long and weighing 21 pounds (9.5 kg), the largest member of its family, it is found at immense depths, down to nearly 9,200 feet (2,800 m).

The poachers (family Agonidae) are completely different in body shape, being long and slim and having a pointed head. The body is usually covered in bony plates, and some species have bristle- or whiskerlike growths on the snout. The best example is the sturgeon poacher (*Podothecus accipenserinus*), a 12-inch (30-cm) species from the North Pacific in which the bristles are bright yellow in color.

While many poacher species can be found in very shallow water—for example, the rockhead (*Bothragonus swanii*), which only extends down to around 60 feet (18 m)—some can dive and live at depths of over 3,280 feet (1,000 m). Poachers are small or relatively small fish, the smallest species being the pixie poacher (*Occella impi*) from the North Pacific, believed to grow to just 0.8 inch (2 cm). Largest of all is the dragon poacher (*Percis japonica*)—again from the North Pacific, which attains a length of 16.5 inches (42 cm).

## Sea Ravens and Other Names

The family Hemitripteridae contains nine species with bodies covered in tiny spines. Among them are two species known as sea ravens, one nearly twice the size of the other. *Hemitripterus americanus* is a northeastern Atlantic species that grows to around 25 inches (64 cm) and is also known by a variety of other names, including the muddler, the bullhead, the cabezón (both names also used for other species), the gurnet, the puff-belly (it inflates when brought to the surface), the web sculpin, the whip sculpin, the whippy, and wip. The other sea raven (*H. villosus*) does not have any alternative common names. At about 14 inches (35 cm) long, it occurs in the North Pacific.

In two of the species—the silver-spotted sculpin (*Blepsias cirrhosus*) from the North Pacific and the sailfin sculpin (*Nautichthys*

---

# Light-boned "Heavyweights"

Although the Baikal oilfish are very light-boned, there are so many of these fish in Baikal Lake that their total weight is estimated to be around 150,000 tons! They are not, however, regarded as food fish. One reason may be their relatively small size—about 6.3 inches (16 cm) in the case of the smaller species and 8.3 inches (21 cm) in the larger one. More significantly, though, these species, despite their vast numbers, do not shoal, making commercial fishing difficult and expensive.

However, the body oil, which can account for as much as 35 percent of the total body weight, is very rich in vitamin A. It is said that in earlier times, when large numbers were washed up along the shores, they would be melted down and their oil used to treat a whole list of ailments, from dressing wounds to rheumatism.

---

*oculofasciatus*) from the northeastern Pacific—the first few spines of the dorsal fin are much larger than the rest. Particularly in the sailfin sculpin these spines are almost half the length of the body, giving it an impressive "horned" appearance when the fish extends its dorsal fin.

## Just One Species

The family Bathylutichthyidae, like the family Rhamphocottidae, contains just one species—(*Bathylutichthys taranetzi*)—that is found only around South Georgia Island in the Antarctic. Like many sculpins, it has a tremendous depth range and is found as deep as 5,415 feet (1,650 m). The only known specimen measured 4 inches (10 cm) in length and had the dorsal, caudal, and anal fins joined up; it also had two long barbels on the lower jaw. So little is known of this fish that its relationship to the sculpins is not clear.

*⊕ The sailfin sculpin (Nautichthys oculofasciatus) favors rocky areas down to 360 feet (110 m). It is a nocturnal hunter that is often found in crevices.*

**Lumpsucker (*Cyclopterus lumpus*)**

**Common name** Lumpfish and snailfish

**Families** Cyclopteridae (lumpfish, lumpsucker, and lump), Liparidae (snailfish)

**Subfamilies** Cyclopteridae: Cyclopterinae (lumpfish), Aptocylinae (lumpsucker)

**Order** Scorpaeniformes

**Number of species** Cyclopteridae: 28 in about 8 genera; Liparidae: 195 in about 19 genera

**Size** From 0.8 in (2 cm) to 30 in (77 cm)

**Key features** Stocky, almost globelike bodies (lumpfish) or elongated (snailfish); generally covered in tubercles or lumps (lumpfish), smooth and scaleless (most snailfish); head blunt (lumpfish) or more pointed (snailfish); 2 dorsal fins (lumpfish), front fin covered in skin in members of subfamily Aptocyclinae, or 1 long-based dorsal fin (snailfish) that can join with caudal and anal fins; in most (but not midwater) species (especially snailfish) pelvic fins joined into suction disk that is located in throat area; variable coloration: often subdued browns and grays (lumpfish), some pale in color (snailfish)

**Breeding** Eggs are laid in masses on bottom, guarded by male, and hatch in 2 weeks (many lumpfish); eggs laid on bottom or inside gill cavity of crabs (snailfish), some species incubating eggs inside their mouths

**Diet** Primarily invertebrates, including jellyfish (some lumpfish species); larger species also take fish

**Habitat** Most species bottom-dwellers over mud, sand, or among gravel, rocks, and seaweed; some shallow-water species found in wave-influenced areas and tidal pools; deepwater species of snailfish at depths over 24,600 ft (7,500 m); some snailfish species also occur in midwater

**Distribution** Cooler marine waters of Northern Hemisphere extending into polar regions; also widely distributed from Arctic to Antarctic

⤒ *The 23.6-inch (60-cm) lumpsucker (Cyclopterus lumpus) occurs on both sides of the Atlantic from Canada eastward to Spain.*

# Lumpfish and Snailfish

Cyclopteridae, Liparidae

*Covered in bumps and suckers, and built like underwater tanks, the 28 or so members of the lumpfish family are not the most beautiful of fish, but their eggs make a valuable contribution to the caviar industry.*

TOGETHER THE CYCLOPTERIDAE AND LIPARIDAE families, which are sometimes classified as one family, contain at least 223 species, but this number is continually expanding since many new species of snailfish are known to exist and are awaiting scientific study.

## Lumps and Suckers

Despite their close relationship, lumpfish and snailfish can be distinguished at a glance. The lumpfish, or lumpsuckers, are stockily built fish, almost globe-shaped, whose body is usually covered in tubercles (lumps).

There are usually two small dorsal fins, and most species have pelvic fins (though not all). In those that do have them, the pelvics are joined in the form of a suction disk. These suckers are used to hold on to rocks in the shallow, wave-affected waters where many of these species are found.

Two subfamilies are generally recognized, with the Cyclopteridae differing largely in the nature of the dorsal fin. In the two species that make up the subfamily Aptocyclinae, the first dorsal fin is covered by thick skin.

The smallest of the lumpfish is *Lethotremus awae* (no common name) from Japanese coasts and the area around Chefoo in China; it grows to a little over 0.8 inches (2 cm). The largest is the lumpfish, or lumpsucker (*Cyclopterus lumpus*), also called the lump. This Atlantic species measures about 24 inches (60 cm) in length and weighs between 11 and 21 pounds (5-9 kg). It is the most exploited of all the lumpfish species, with the flesh being sold fresh

⤓ *The lumpsucker (Cyclopterus lumpus) earns its name from the way in which it uses its pelvic fins to form a suction pad with which it can cling to a rock or other appropriate surface.*

or smoked, especially in Scandinavia, while its eggs (roe) are sold either fresh or prepared as lumpfish caviar, which (although less expensive than the sturgeon equivalent) is worth well over $10 million per year.

## Jelly and Suckers

The snailfish (family Liparidae) look very different from the lumpfish. They are long, scaleless fish with jellylike skin that feels as if it fits loosely on the underlying muscle layers.

Where the lumpfish tend to have two small dorsal fins, the snailfish only have one, with a very long base stretching from behind the head all the way to the tail, which it sometimes joins. The anal fin, too, may join with the tail.

At the moment there are around 195 species in about 19 genera of snailfish. Most of them have suckerlike pelvic fins, one of several characteristics showing their relationship with the lumpsuckers. However, all the members of the genus *Paraliparis* and the tadpole snailfish

(*Nectoliparis pelagicus*)—the single species of its genus—lack this feature.

Despite not being often seen, the deepwater species of snailfish are among the most successful of all such species; some, like *Pseudoliparis belyaevi* (no common name), can occur at depths of over 24,600 feet (7,500 m) and are distributed all the way from the Arctic to the Antarctic Ocean. One factor that is thought to have contributed to this deepwater success is that it appears the larvae of these snailfish (or liparids) are not planktonic but benthic—in other words, bottom-living. If we add also the family's long history of living in cold, deep waters, that may account for the gradual but extensive spread of deepwater species of snailfish over time.

Some species live in extremely shallow water. Typical of this group is the tidepool snailfish (*Liparis florae*), a 7-inch (18-cm) species from the Eastern Pacific that lives on exposed coasts.

# Flatfish

Fish are beautifully symmetrical—one side of the body is an identical mirror image of the other side. There are a few exceptions, however, like the one-sided livebearers (*Jenynsia* species) in which parts of the anal fin are slanted, but only slightly, to one side, or some of the spikefish (family Tricanthodidae) in which the snout twists to the left or right with advancing age. The best-known asymmetrical fish, however, are the various species of flatfish.

## Order Pleuronectiformes: 2 suborders, 11 families, about 123 genera, 693 species

**Suborder** Pleuronectoidei—10 families, about 122 genera, and 690 species

    **Families** Citharidae—citharids; Bothidae—lefteye flounders*; Achiropsettidae—southern flounders; Scophthalmidae—scophthalmids; Paralichthyidae—large-tooth flounders; Pleuronectidae—righteye flounders**; Samaridae; Achiridae—American soles; Soleidae—soles; Cynoglossidae—tongue soles or tonguefish***

    * THE BOTHIDAE ARE DIVIDED INTO 2 SUBFAMILIES:

        • BOTHINAE—AT LEAST 13 GENERA AND 135 SPECIES

        • TAENIOPSETTINAE—AT LEAST 2 GENERA AND 4 SPECIES

    ** THE PLEURONECTIDAE ARE USUALLY DIVIDED INTO 4 SUBFAMILIES:

        • PLEURONECTINAE—FURTHER SUBDIVIDED INTO 2 TRIBES:

            + HIPPOGLOSSINI—CONTAINING THE HALIBUTS (*HYPPOLOSSUS* SPECIES) AND THEIR RELATIVES IN 10 GENERA AND ABOUT 20 SPECIES

            + PLEURONECTINI—CONTAINING THE EUROPEAN PLAICE (*PLEURONECTES PLATESSA*) AND RELATIVES IN AROUND 21 GENERA AND 60 SPECIES

        • PARALICHTHODINAE—1 SPECIES, THE PEPPERED FLOUNDER (*PARALICHTHODES ALGRENSIS*)

        • POECILOPSETTINAE—3 GENERA AND AROUND 19 SPECIES: FOR EXAMPLE, THE NARROW-BODY RIGHTEYE FLOUNDER (*NEMATOPS CHUI*) AND RELATIVES

        • RHOMBOSOLEINAE—9 GENERA AND AROUND 19 SPECIES: FOR EXAMPLE, THE INDONESIAN OCELLATED FLOUNDER (*PSAMMODISCUS OCELLATUS*) AND RELATIVES

    *** THE CYNOGLOSSIDAE ARE DIVIDED INTO 2 SUBFAMILIES:

        • SYMPHURINAE—1 GENUS AND ABOUT 66 SPECIES: FOR EXAMPLE, NORMAN'S TONGUE SOLE (*SYMPHURUS NORMANI*)

        • CYNOGLOSSINAE—2 GENERA: *CYNOGLOSSUS*, WITH ABOUT 60 SPECIES: FOR EXAMPLE, FRESHWATER TONGUE SOLE (*C. HETEROLEPIS*); AND *PARAPLOGUSIA*, WITH 6 SPECIES, FOR EXAMPLE, LONG-SNOUTED TONGUE SOLE (*P. LONGIROSTRIS*)

**Suborder** Psettodoidei—1 family, 1 genus, and 3 species

    **Family** Psettodidae—psettodids

## Nonflat Flatfish

Flatfish are world famous not only as food fish but also for their habit of appearing to lie flat on the bottom.

Strictly speaking, lying flat implies lying on either the belly or the back, but flatfish do neither. Instead, they lie on their side. For example, the plaice (*Pleuronectes platessa*) lies on its left side (at least, the vast majority of specimens do). The lefteye flounders (family Bothidae) lie

⊕ *The eyes of a flounder (family Pleuronectidae) are close together, but, as the shape of the mouth suggests, they are not on the top of the body but on the side.*

on their right side, while the starry flounder (*Platichthys stellatus*) lies either on its left or on its right.

Despite not lying on their bellies, both eyes appear to be on top of the fish—what appears to be the belly of the fish is white, but its back appears to be darker.

## Masters of Asymmetry

Flatfish are the masters of asymmetry, yet when they are born, they look like the larvae of normal fish. In other words, every part of the body is where it is supposed to be. These larvae also swim as other fish do—in an upright position.

Then something very odd begins to happen. When these tiny fish are normally between 0.04 and 0.1 inches (0.1—0.25 cm) long, one eye begins to migrate across the top of the head onto the other side, ending up close to the other eye.

Once both eyes are on the same side of the head, the young fish can only see from one side of its body. At this point a juvenile flatfish sinks to the bottom and lies on its eyeless side. It also begins to swim in this horizontal position.

However, the transformation from a normal fish to a flatfish is far from complete. Skull bones, muscles, fins, nerves, mouth, teeth, coloration, and other features all gradually undergo changes that make it possible for these fish to live the rest of their lives lying on their side.

## Right-handed versus Left-handed

In the majority of flatfish—there are 11 families, some divided into subfamilies and tribes (see box opposite)—both eyes end up on the right side of the body, which therefore becomes the back. These right-handed species are referred to as "dextral." Those whose eyes migrate to

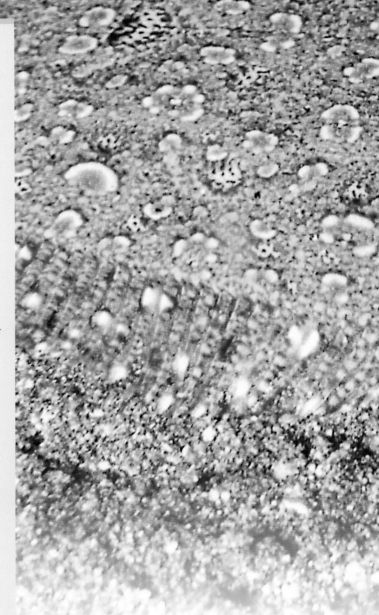

# Now You See Me, Now You Don't

In "normal" fish the back is darker than the belly in all but a few species, like the upside-down catfish (*Synodontis nigriventris*), which, as its name suggests, spends much of its time swimming upside down. Therefore the dark back is directed toward the surface of the water, and the light-colored belly is directed downward, toward the bottom, in all but a few exceptions to this rule.

But in flatfish the "back" is, in reality, one of the sides of the body, while the "belly" is the other side. Therefore it is not surprising to find that in the course of evolution, the upper side has developed the darker colors that other fish have on their backs, and the lower side has become light or white, just like the belly in "normal" fish.

This arrangement is perfectly suited to the lifestyle of these fish, which spend their time on, or buried in, the bottom. Usually the top side has a mottled pattern that tends to blend in with the surroundings, thus offering them some protection from predators. However, such mottled patterning only provides camouflage as long as it matches the immediate surroundings. Once the flatfish moves away and onto a differently colored patch of bottom, it will stand out unless it buries itself completely, or unless it changes its color.

Flatfish do both—they are expert burrowers as well as fishy "chameleons." They can bury themselves in a matter of just a few seconds by vigorously undulating their bodies in a swiminglike movement, but without moving forward or backward. Once they are buried, only the eyes project above the surface, thus making the flatfish very difficult to spot from above.

the left side of the head are known as "sinistral" species.

It would be logical if this rule were to apply throughout the whole order (Pleuronectiformes) of flatfish, but nature does not work like that.

The psettotids (family Psettodidae), for example, contains just three species, members of which can be either dextral or sinistral. In the citharids (family Citharidae) there are four genera—two are dextral and

two sinistral. However, in the aptly named lefteye flounders (family Bothidae) all 20 genera are sinistral, while in the righteye flounders (family Pleuronectidae) the 39 or so genera are almost always dextral.

This flexibility, more pronounced in some families, genera, and species than in others, runs throughout the order. Right-handedness or left-handedness is therefore something that, although genetically controlled, is not

⊕ *The panther flounder (Bothus pantherinus) is almost invisible in the sand, while its eyes keep watch for potential prey. It frequents the coral reefs of the west and central Pacific Ocean.*

absolutely fixed in exactly the same way for every individual within every population of every species, genus, or family. Of course, in terms of survival it does not make any difference.

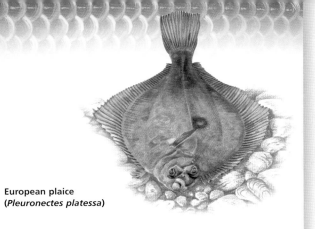

European plaice
(*Pleuronectes platessa*)

**Common name** Flounders

**Families** Bothidae (lefteye flounders),
Pleuronectidae (righteye flounders)

**Subfamilies** Bothidae: Bothinae and Taeniopsettinae;
Pleuronectidae: Pleuronectinae, Rhombosoleinae,
Poecilopsettinae, and Paralichthodinae

**Order** Pleuronectiformes

**Number of species** Bothidae: about 157 in 20 genera;
Pleuronectidae: nearly 120 in about 44 genera

**Size** From 1.4 in (3.5 cm) to 8.5 ft (2.6 m)

**Key features** Asymmetrical, oval-shaped bodies; head with
both eyes on same (top) side; front edge of
dorsal fin located above or in front of eyes; all
fins separate from each other; pelvic fins
asymmetrical in lefteyes, symmetrical in
righteyes; coloration: top side heavily patterned
in many species; capable of rapid color changes

**Breeding** About 2 million eggs released

**Diet** Invertebrates; larger species also take fish

**Habitat** Nearly always marine; Bothidae: tropical and
temperate zones; usually over fine-grained
bottoms; shallow or relatively shallow waters,
normally above 330 ft (100 m); Pleuronectidae:
tropical, subtropical, temperate, and (almost)
arctic zones; usually over fine-grained bottoms;
depths above 660 ft (200 m); some species may
enter brackish water

**Distribution** Atlantic, Indian, and Pacific Oceans;
Pleuronectidae: also Arctic Ocean

**Status** World Conservation Union lists Atlantic halibut
(*Hippoglossus hippoglossus*) as Endangered and
yellowtail flounder (*Limanda ferriginea*) as
Vulnerable

⊕ *The bony ridge of this 40-inch (1-m) European plaice
(Pleuronectes platessa) is visible behind its eyes. Lying flat on the
rocky bottom of very shallow brackish or marine waters, it hunts
for its favorite mollusks at night.*

# Flounders

Bothidae, Pleuronectidae

*The righteye flounders, with few exceptions, have both
eyes on the right side of the head and are most
familiar to us on our plates. Of course, the reverse is
true of the aptly named lefteye flounders.*

TOGETHER THE LEFTEYE FLOUNDERS (FAMILY Bothidae)
and their right-eyed counterparts (family
Pleuronectidae) account for nearly 280 of the
690 or so species that make up the order of
flatfish (Pleuronectiformes). At around 157
species the lefteye flounders are the largest of
the families. The righteye flounders, with 120
species, rank third, being slightly outnumbered
by the tonguefish family (Cynoglossidae), at
around 135 species in just three genera.

## Fish on the Menu

Most of the best-known species that are fished
commercially for food are righteye flounders,
but there are also some familiar types not just
among the lefteye flounders but also members
of other families (see box).

Usually flatfish are caught in trawl nets
over fine-grained bottoms at varying depths
depending on species and time of year. Some,
such as the Atlantic halibut (*Hippoglossus
hippoglossus*), can be found at great depths—
from around 165 feet (50 m) down to around
6,560 feet (2,000 m). The Pacific halibut

⊕ *The eyed flounder
(Bothus ocellatus) is
found in the Indian and
West Pacific Oceans.*

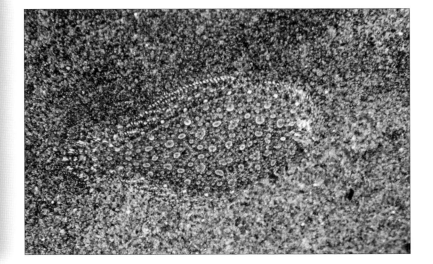

(*H. stenolepis*) does not extend to such great depths but can still be found at around 3,610 feet (1,100 m). Both fish are highly commercial and are usually caught at considerably shallower depths than their maximum.

In the past the Atlantic halibut has been fished very heavily, to such an extent that now the World Conservation Union officially lists it as Endangered. With dwindling stocks and the continuing high demand for this excellent food fish, several experimental projects aimed at rearing the species under controlled conditions have met with some success.

The commercial breeding of European plaice (*Pleuronectes platessa*) is far better established, and important quantities of farmed stocks are now available. It is not endangered, and demand has led to captive rearing.

Soles are also popular food fish, with the lemon sole (*Microstomus kitt*) and Dover sole being particularly highly regarded in international cuisine. However, the Dover sole enjoyed by European diners is quite distinct from that consumed in the U.S. The European Dover sole is *Solea solea*, which can grow to 24 inches (60 cm). It is not a member of the Pleuronectidae or Bothidae (the two families discussed here) but of the Soleidae (discussed under "Soles"). In the U.S. the American Dover sole is *M. pacificus*, a larger fish at around 30 inches (76 cm); it is a member of the Pleuronectidae along with the lemon sole, itself a sizable fish at 26 inches (65 cm) long.

Undoubtedly, the leading species is the European plaice, a northeastern Atlantic species that can grow to around 40 inches (100 cm), weighs around 15.5 pounds (7 kg), and can live for up to 50 years. Few people, though, ever get to see any specimens even closely approaching this size, weight, and age.

⬆ *The European plaice (Pleuronectes platessa) is distinguished by the orange spots on one side of its body, while the other side is characteristically pale. Plaice tend to move from relatively shallow water to deeper water as they grow older.*

The vast majority seen in food markets are less than half this size and are nowhere near the age limit for the species. This species is the most important flatfish in Europe and is sold both fresh and frozen in large quantities.

Adult European plaice can be found in waters as deep as 650 feet (200 m). Although adults can also be found in very shallow water, most of the specimens encountered in such habitats are small. Few, if any, small individuals are ever encountered at depth.

### Other Popular Flounders and Friends

While the species mentioned above are among the best-known and most popular flatfish that are eaten in many countries, numerous other species (belonging to several families) are also consumed, some in large quantities. In fact, there are probably more members of this order that are regarded as food fish than of most others. The brill (*Scophthalmus rhombus*), for example, is a 30-inch (75-cm), 16-pound (7.2-kg) European, Mediterranean, and Black Sea member of the family Scophthalmidae, with a broad body and delicate flesh that is popular mainly (but not exclusively) in the more northern European regions.

Another member of this family, the topknot (*Zeugopterus punctatus*), is even more northern in its distribution and is popular in Britain and parts of Scandinavia.

The dab (*Limanda limanda*) is also a predominantly northern Atlantic species. It can grow to 17 inches (42 cm) and weighs around 2.8 pounds (1.3 kg). The flounder (*Pleuronectes flesus*) is longer and heavier, and extends further south to the Moroccan coast and into the Mediterranean and Baltic Seas. Both are members of the family Pleuronectidae that enjoy considerable popularity.

Along the Pacific Coast of the U.S. many species of flatfish are taken both as game and food fish. They include the Pacific sanddab (*Cithraichthys sordidus*) and the California flounder (*Paralichthys californicus*) from the large-tooth flounder family (Paralichthyidae)—plus several members of the righteye flounder family, including the rex sole (*Glyptocephalus zachirus*) and the petrale sole (*Eopsetta jordani*). In the more northern regions the rock sole (*Lepidopsetta bilineata*) is fished in large numbers, while the English sole (*Parophrys*

## The Fishing Flatfish

**A**ll flatfish are predators and tend to ambush their prey. However, the angler flatfish (*Asterorhombus fijiensis*) in the family Bothidae takes matters a significant step further and actually fishes for its food. It has a form of built-in fishing rod with a bait or lure that, through the remarkable process of "parallel" evolution, closely resembles the "rod and lure" arrangement found in the angler fish (order Lophiiformes).

This 6-inch (15-cm) Indo-Pacific species is found in shallow tropical waters, often on coral sandy bottoms at depths of less than 100 feet (30 m). There it lies motionless, partly covered or camouflaged and thus invisible to its potential prey. One part of the body, though, is very visible—the rodlike first spine of the dorsal fin and its modified tip that looks like a small shrimp. The angler flatfish waves this rod and lure (called the "ilicium" and "esca," respectively) in the water until an unsuspecting victim becomes attracted by the "shrimp." However, this "shrimp" is no meal, as the would-be predator dramatically discovers when the flatfish sucks it into its large mouth in a lightning-fast move.

⊕ *The dab (Limanda limanda) feeds largely on crustaceans and small fish, and can be found at depths down to 490 feet (150 m). It is native to the northeast Atlantic and the Baltic Sea.*

*vetulus*) is similarly fished from British Columbia down to California.

Among the Asian species the pelican flounder (*Chascanopsetta lugubris*) of the family Bothidae is one of the more unusual-looking food species. It grows to nearly 16 inches (40 cm) and occurs at depths of between 200 and 3,300 feet (60–1,000 m). It has a large mouth with a saclike throat, hence the name pelican. This huge gape allows it to feed on large prey.

The above is a small selection of the many species of flatfish that are consumed in various regions. Though markets and demands may vary, the vast majority of these fish are sold either fresh or frozen. Some, though, are dried, salted, or ground into fishmeal, while a few, such as the butter sole (*Isopsetta isolepis*) and the American Dover sole, are also sold for feeding to captive-reared mink on fur farms.

## Lefteyes and Righteyes Compared

Apart from the fact that the lefteye and righteye flounders can, with few exceptions, be told apart—depending on which side of the head the eyes are located—there appear to be few other easily observed differences between the members of these families. Indeed, some scientists think that the righteye flounders of the subfamily Pleuronectinae resemble the lefteye flounders more closely than they do the members of the other subfamilies within their own family.

The fact is that at first sight, members of both the lefteye and righteye families look remarkably similar and share similar lifestyles. For example, the dorsal fin in both starts far forward on the body, above or in front of the eyes. They also both have their dorsal and anal fins quite separate from the tail, and so on.

Indeed, it is only when we start looking at smaller details, like the presence or absence of oil globules in the eggs and relative lengths of the pelvic fins, that distinct differences begin to appear. It is not surprising, therefore, that opinions differ among scientists on how these families should be identified, or if the subfamily of righteye flounders, which contains the European plaice, the halibuts, and around 40 other species, are really righteye flounders or special types of lefteye flounder.

**Drab sole (*Achirus achirus*)**

**Common name** Soles

**Families** Soleidae (soles), Achiridae (American soles), Cynoglossidae (tongue soles or tonguefish)

**Subfamilies** Cynoglossidae: Symphurinae and Cynoglossinae

**Order** Pleuronectiformes

**Number of species** Soleidae: over 120 in 26 genera; Achiridae: around 28 in 9 genera; Cynoglossidae: about 135 in 3 genera

**Size** From 0.8 inches (2 cm) to 43.3 in (110 cm)

**Key features** Oval-shaped bodies: from slim to relatively circular; asymmetrical with both eyes on same side of head; dorsal and anal fins very long-based; caudal fin separate in soles and American soles, continuous with dorsal and anal in tongue soles; pectoral fins absent in tongue soles; coloration: top side usually mottled or banded in various colors; bottom side white or light-colored

**Breeding** Eggs and sperm released into water, then abandoned

**Die** Invertebrates; also fish

**Habitat** Soleidae: tropical to temperate zones; shallow or relatively shallow seas; some species inhabit deep water down to 4,430 ft (1,350 m), others in marine and brackish waters, a few in fresh water (especially fine-grained bottoms); Achiridae: tropical to temperate zones; primarily over fine-grained bottoms; most species marine, but many in brackish waters or fresh water; Cynoglossidae: tropical and subtropical zones; mainly deepwater marine and predominantly shallow water, from marine though brackish to fresh water

**Distribution** Soleidae: mainly European, African, Asian, and Australian seas; Achiridae: mostly both coasts of North and South America, also Indonesia, Australia, New Guinea, perhaps the Philippines; Cynoglossinae: most seas; not Arctic or Antarctic

⤢ *The 7.1-in (18-cm) drab sole (Achirus achirus), found on sandy or muddy bottoms of estuaries, rivers, and coastal streams, hides itself completely in sediment, leaving only its eyes visible.*

# Soles

Soleidae, Achiridae, Cynoglossidae

*The European Dover sole grows well beyond the "plate size" that we usually associate with it. In fact, it can grow to nearly 28 inches (70 cm) in length and live for about 27 years.*

CONFUSINGLY, WHILE THE EUROPEAN DOVER sole (*Solea solea*), also known as the common sole, belongs to the family Soleidae, the American Dover sole (*Microstomus pacificus*) belongs to the righteye flounder family (Pleuronectidae) dealt with previously in this book.

## Flexible Americans

Even more confusing, the group known generally as American soles belongs to the family Achiridae. Despite their name, not all 28 American soles occur in either North or South America. For example, the estuary sole (*Achirus poropterus*) is found in Indonesia, New Guinea, and northern Australia, and possibly in the Philippines. It is an inshore species that is found mainly in estuaries and the lower parts of freshwater streams. It never extends more than a mile or so (1.6 km) inland, unlike some of its relatives—certainly unlike the freshwater saltpan sole (*Synaptura salinarum*) or the even more impressive hogchoker (*Trinectes maculatus*). This 8-inch (20-cm) American sole is a western Atlantic species; it occurs either in coastal waters to a depth of 245 feet (75 m) or in estuaries, sometimes several hundreds of miles upriver.

The drab sole (*A. achirus*) is also sometimes referred to as the American freshwater sole or flatfish; it can grow to around 7 inches (18 cm). It is an estuarine and freshwater species that is found in tropical waters from Venezuela to northeastern Brazil. Its unusual habit is to hang from the undersurface of the water (using its surface tension properties). It can also form an almost complete suction disk by pressing the underside of its body against a surface to stick to rocks and other hard objects, especially in

⊙ *The Dover sole (Solea solea) blends with its sandy environment. It is found around the coasts of Britain and Ireland at depths between 32.8 and 197 feet (10–60 m). The rounded head and small, downturned mouth are distinctive features.*

# Versatile Habitats

In total there are about 26 genera of soles (Soleidae) with just over 120 species. Most are found in shallow or relatively shallow water, but some, most notably the deepwater sole (*Bathysolea profundicola*), an 8-in (20-cm) species from the eastern Atlantic, can occur at great depths. This commercial species is found at depths varying from 820 to 4,430 feet (250–1,350 m); it is not, of course, fished at the lower end of its depth range.

In terms of salinity a majority of species are strictly marine. However, some predominantly marine species are considerably more flexible and occur in both marine and brackish waters. Klein's sole (*Synaptura kleinii*) and several of the zebra soles (*Zebrais* species) are among these adaptable species.

At the other end of the spectrum several species are entirely (or almost entirely) confined to fresh water, the most extreme example of these being the saltpan sole (*Synaptura salinarum*), which can be found hundreds of miles inland in the freshwater rivers of the Gulf of Carpentaria drainage in the north of Australia.

The most versatile soles of all, though, can tolerate the full range of water conditions from freshwater through brackish to marine. One of the most adaptable of all is *Synaptura lusitanica nigromaculata*, a west African species.

flowing waters. This sole is the only one kept in any numbers by aquarists—for its interesting body patterns, behavior, and the relative ease with which it can be kept.

The flexibility or ability to adapt to various types of habitat is an important factor that the drab sole shares with its European relative, the common sole (family Soleidae). Both these sole families share very closely related ancestors. The earliest fossils of both familes occur in Lower Eocene rocks dating back 60 million years.

## Migrating Sole

Along with the European plaice (*Pleuronectes platessa*) and the two halibuts (*Hippoglossus* species) covered earlier in this book the common sole is in high demand throughout (and outside) its range. It extends from around Trondheim in Norway southward to the coast of Senegal in Africa and eastward into the Mediterranean and parts of the Black Sea.

Such is the demand that wild harvests of the common sole, like the European plaice, are now widely backed up by stocks farmed in ponds in several European countries. Owing to its substantial size and predatory nature, it is

# American Sole or Common Sole?

Like their more numerous cousins, the American soles (family Achiridae) have both eyes on the right side of the head. Generally speaking, though, they are smaller, more rounded fish.

On closer examination other differences begin to appear; perhaps the two most easily distinguishable of them are the mouth and the pelvic fin on the eyed (top) side. The lower lip on this side has a fleshy rim with a fringe on it that is lacking in the common sole family (Soleidae). The pelvic fin of the eyed side is different in that in the American soles, it is joined to the anal fin by a membrane, while in the common soles it is quite separate.

Other differences are more subtle and can only be detected by a study of the skeleton, particularly the skull. This has led most scientists to conclude that although American soles are very similar to common soles, they are not sufficiently similar to belong to the same family. However, really detailed study of the present nine genera and 28 species show that matters are not quite so straightforward as this. Interesting changes, therefore, await this group in the near future.

fish's overall shape—much slimmer than soles and, in turn, slimmer than American soles.

Three features immediately separate the tongue soles from their closest relatives. First of all, the eyes are on the left side of the head—in the other two families they are on the right. Second, the dorsal, caudal, and anal fins are all joined, but in soles and American soles they are quite separate. Finally, these tongue soles do not have pectoral fins.

There are only three genera of tongue sole, but about 135 species. Two of the genera—*Symphurus* and *Cynoglossus*—contain 69 and 61 species, respectively, while the remaining genus, *Paraplagusia*, contains just six.

Despite there being so few genera, one of them is so distinct and the other two so similar that two subfamilies have been created to accommodate them. The Symphurinae contains the 69 species of *Symphurus* with their almost straight mouth located at the tip of the snout. Members of this subfamily are generally deepwater flatfish, occurring at depths from

also considered a good game fish despite its mainly night-time feeding habits.

Although the common sole is a typical bottom-dwelling flatfish throughout most of the year, it undertakes spawning migrations during which it swims in groups well clear of the bottom, frequently just under the surface. Spawning takes place in shallow water, with up to 100,000 eggs being released. In typical flatfish fashion the eggs take about ten days to hatch. Newly hatched larvae are normal in that they have one eye on either side of the body, normally distributed fins, and so on. When they reach 0.5 inch (1.3 cm), they settle on the bottom, having already begun their remarkable transformation into asymmetrical flatfish.

## Tongue-shaped Relatives

In addition to American soles (family Achiridae) and soles (family Soleidae) there is a third family of sole—the tongue soles (family Cynoglossidae)—more frequently referred to as tonguefish. Both common names arise from the

*⤴ The saltpan sole (Synaptura salinarum) has an elongated, somewhat oval-shaped body and is found in slow-moving, fresh or brackish waters.*

*⬅ The small-headed sole (Soleichthys microcephalus) has distinctive yellow-and-black bands on its body. These colors may act as a warning to any potential predator.*

around 985 feet (300 m) down to some 6,235 feet (1,900 m).

## Shallow-water Species

In marked contrast, the majority of the members of the Cynoglossinae are shallow-water species, but some are even found in fresh water. These fish have a hooked snout with the mouth located on its underside—the "right" side of their head when the fish is viewed from the front.

As is the case with their relatives in the two other families, several tonguefish are also important food fish, including the largest species of all—Norman's tongue sole (*Symphurus normani*). It is an eastern Atlantic shallow-water species that grows to around 27.5 inches (70 cm) and is found at depths between 165 and 330 feet (50–100 m). The smallest species—the patchtail tongue sole (*S. rhytisma*) from the west-central Atlantic—grows to around 1.6 inches (4 cm) in length, but it is of no commercial interest.

# Triggers, Puffers, and Relatives

Order Tetraodontiformes

Although they cannot match many other orders in terms of numbers, the triggerfish, puffers, and their allies more than make up for this in their unexpected and weird adaptations. These fish have feeding and body modifications that few other orders can match, especially modestly sized ones, making them one of the most fascinating groups of fish on the planet.

## Pincushions and Twisted Noses

The longsnout spikefish (family Tricanthodidae) have powerful spines and a long snout that becomes twisted to the left or right with age. The porcupinefish (family Diodontidae) are like an inflatable, living pincushion. The triggerfish (family Balistidae) have lockable dorsal fins and prey on sea urchins, while their close relatives, the filefish (family Monacanthidae), have skin like sandpaper.

There are also triplespines (family Triacanthidae) that resemble triggerfish but behave totally differently; armor-plated boxfish and cowfish with "horns" (family Ostraciontidae); various puffers (families Triodontidae and Tetraodontidae) with fused teeth that can easily crunch snail shells; as well as gigantic molas (family Molidae) that look like ocean-roaming fish "gone wrong."

Yet for all their differences in size, shape, and habits, all 410 or so species are generally regarded as belonging to a single order of fish—the Tetraodontiformes (also sometimes called Plectognathi). As with other orders of fish, scientists have different opinions on how various groups relate to each other—especially with triplespines and spikefish, generally considered the most primitive members of the nine families usually placed in the order.

Several features of the skull, skeleton, and muscle arrangements are characteristics shared by most members of the order. For example, most species do not have lower ribs or several of the nose and eye bones; the upper jaw is usually fused to the bone that lies in front of it (premaxilla). Also, most species have modified body scales in the form of plates, shields, or spines, and so on.

There are so many variations within the fishes' overall framework that it is likely there will be important changes in their future classification. However, here the puffers, triggers, and relatives are split into nine families:

## Spikefish and Triplespines

These two families are generally regarded as the two most primitive ones within the order and are discussed in the next entry.

The two groups have many variations but share two significant characteristics—spikes or spines—as reflected in their common names. Both their dorsal and pelvic fins

---

Order Tetraodontiformes: 2 suborders, 9 families, about 107 genera, around 410 species:

**Suborder** Triacanthoidei—2 families, about 15 genera, and 28 species

**Families** Triacanthodidae—spikefish*; Triacanthidae—triplespines

* THE TRIACANTHODIDAE ARE SOMETIMES DIVIDED INTO 2 SUBFAMILIES:

• HOLLARDIINAE—RETICULATE SPIKEFISH (HOLLARDIA HOLLARDI) AND 4 RELATIVES

• TRIACANTHODINAE—LONGSNOUT SPIKEFISH (HALIMOCHIRURGUS CENTRISCOIDES) AND 15 OTHER SPECIES

**Suborder** Tetraodontoidei—7 families, about 92 genera, and about 382 species

**Families** Balistidae—triggerfish**; Monacanthidae—filefish**; Ostraciidae or Ostraciontidae—boxfish, trunkfish, and cowfish***; Triodontidae—three-toothed puffer or pursefish; Tetraodontidae—puffers****; Diodontidae—porcupinefish or burrfish; Molidae—molas or ocean sunfish

** THE BALISTIDAE AND MONACANTHIDAE ARE REGARDED AS SUBFAMILIES IN SOME CLASSIFICATIONS: IN OTHER WORDS, BALISTINAE AND MONACANTHINAE, RESPECTIVELY

*** THE OSTRACIIDAE IS USUALLY DIVIDED INTO 2 SUBFAMILIES (CONSIDERED AS FULL FAMILIES BY SOME AUTHORS):

• ARACANINAE—STRIPED COWFISH (ARACANA AURITA) AND ABOUT 12 RELATIVES

• OSTRACIINAE—BOXFISH: FOR EXAMPLE., OSTRACION; SOME COWFISH: FOR EXAMPLE, LACTORIA AND RELATIVES (ABOUT 20 SPECIES IN TOTAL)

**** THE TETRAODONTIDAE ARE USUALLY DIVIDED INTO 2 SUBFAMILIES:

• TETRAODONTINAE—THE "NORMAL" PUFFERS

• CANTHIGASTRINAE—SHARPNOSE PUFFERS; 1 GENUS: CANTHIGASTER

have prominent spines that (in the pelvics) can be locked in a raised position. The triplespines are shallow-water fish, while spikefish occur in deep to very deep water.

### Triggers and Filefish

The triggerfish and filefish, like the spikefish and triplespines (described above), also have lockable fin spines. In their case it is the dorsal fin (not the pelvic) that can be locked by a trigger mechanism that makes it almost impossible to lower this fin by force.

Triggers and filefish use this defense strategy in various ways—the most effective is to wedge themselves inside a crevice. Once in this position, they are extremely difficult to dislodge, especially when they also raise their pelvic spine and skin flap, to such an extent that most predators will give up to look for easier prey.

### Boxfish and Cowfish

In terms of pelvic fins the boxfish and cowfish go one stage further than the triggers and filefish—they do not even have a pelvic spine.

However, their body is encased in armor, which restricts their movements but gives them very effective protection. These fish also have a hidden weapon in the form of a powerful poison that they can release when alarmed or under attack. It is so potent that when released into a confined space like an aquarium, it can kill the other fish. Incredibly, the boxfish and cowfish are not themselves immune to their own toxin.

### Puffers and Porcupines

The three families that form this group have fused teeth—two in Diodontidae (porcupinefish) and, for puffers, three in Triodontidae and four in Tetraodontidae.

These species also inflate or puff up their bodies with water, giving predators a difficult-to-handle

⊖ *Not only can the tasseled filefish (Chaetodermis penicilligerus) camouflage itself with its seaweed-looking tassels, it can also wedge itself into a suitable crevice from which it is difficult for a predator to dislodge it, especially if the fish raises its pelvic spine and skin flap.*

mouthful. In the case of porcupinefish this defense is made even more effective by the presence of numerous body spines. Like the boxfish, many puffers are poisonous. However, they do not release poison but carry it within their body tissues, gut, or organs.

### Ocean Sunfish

The molas, or ocean sunfish, are the giants of the order—some of the largest specimens measure over 6.6 feet (2 m) and weigh well over 2,000 pounds (1,000 kg). They are gentle fish living in open waters and are famous not just for their size but for the lack of a tail, which gives them an "unfinished" look.

Shortsnout spikefish
(*Triacanthodes ethiops*)

**Common name** Spikefish and triplespines

**Families** Triacanthodidae (spikefish), Triacanthidae (triplespines or tripodfish)

**Subfamilies** Triacanthodidae: Hollardiinae, Triacanthodinae

**Order** Tetraodontiformes

**Number of species** Triacanthodidae: about 21 in 11 genera; Triacanthidae: 7 in 4 genera

**Size** From 2 in (5 cm) to 12 in (30 cm)

**Key features** Elongated to deep body or deep at front, tapering to narrow caudal peduncle at back; some have long snouts with small mouths at tip, snout twisted to left or right; deep-bodied forms have small mouths, lack snouts; some have pointed head, small mouth at tip; eyes generally large, in some species set high on skull; prominent spines on dorsal fin, one on pelvic fin can be locked when raised; rounded tail fin or deeply forked; coloration: reddish or reddish-brown, fading to lighter color on belly; some have one or more thin bluish lines running along body (spikefish); usually silvery gray overlaid with other colors along top of body, also yellow or green marks and black patch on dorsal fin's base (triplespines)

**Breeding** Eggs and sperm of triplespines released or scattered, then abandoned; larvae spend time among plankton; spines develop when larvae are 0.15 in (0.4 cm) long or at earlier stage

**Diet** Long-snouted species: soft, bottom-dwelling invertebrates (e.g., worms); "spoon-toothed": fish scales; also hard-shelled invertebrates (e.g., crustaceans) and bottom-living invertebrates

**Habitat** Shallow coastal waters down to about 360 ft (110 m), usually above 215 ft (65 m), or deep tropical, subtropical marine waters, down to 6,600 ft (2,000 m); some species in brackish water; longsnouted species over fine-grained bottoms; also sandy, muddy areas

**Distribution** Western Atlantic and Indo-Pacific

⤒ *The 3.3-inch (8.5-cm) shortsnout spikefish (Triacanthodes ethiops) is found in tropical waters at depths between 164 and 410 feet (50–125 m) in the Indo-West Pacific from South Africa eastward to Japan and south to Australia.*

# Spikefish and Triplespines

Triacanthodidae,
Triacanthidae

*The spikefish family has some weird and wonderful types, with long, twisted snouts and spoon-shaped teeth. Many species have to endure the astronomical pressures of living at great depths.*

THE SPIKEFISH FORM THE FAMILY Triacanthodidae, which contains around 21 species in 11 genera. They are very varied in shape—from slim, long-snouted types, like the aptly named longsnout spikefish (*Halimochirurgus centriscoides*) and trumpetsnout spikefish (*Macrorhamphosodes platycheilus*) in the subfamily Tricanthodinae to deep-bodied, normal-snouted forms like the reticulate spikefish (*Hollardia hollardi*) in the subfamily Hollardiinae.

## Little-known Spikefish

Although museum specimens are available, and the skeletal features of spikefish, therefore, have been relatively well studied, little is known about the lives of these mainly deepwater fish. For example, how is the long snout used, and why, in older specimens, is it twisted? Does this twisting ever progress to the extent that the snout becomes of little use to the fish?

One of the factors that influences the search for knowledge about these fish is that most species are found in deep water—from around 330 feet (100 m) down to over 6,500 feet (2,000 m). Some, including the long-snouted species, are known to occur over mudflats. So, with the mouth located at the tip of the snout and with only a few, small, widely spaced teeth, this could indicate that these fish feed on soft, bottom-dwelling invertebrates, such as worms.

In the trumpetsnout species the mouth is at the tip of the snout, as with longsnouts. However, the tooth arrangement is totally different. The two trumpetsnouts have spoon-shaped teeth on the lower jaw that press against a thick pad of tissue on the upper jaw when the mouth is closed. This arrangement allows them to scrape off scales from the bodies of other fish.

The fleshy-lipped spikefish (*Tydemania navigatoris*) does not have a trumpetlike snout, but its mouth and tooth arrangement also make it a scale-eater. In contrast, studies of the stomach contents of some of the more massively built species have revealed mollusk and crustacean fragments. The spikefish family therefore appears to have a wide-ranging diet.

Linking all 21 members of this diverse group together are several features of the skeleton. The most significant (or most easily seen) ones are the dorsal fin's heavily spined front part, as well as the long spine in their pelvic fin—hence their family name. The pelvic fin spine can also be locked into position at an outwardly pointing angle, making spikefish a painful mouthful for any would-be predator.

## Spiky Relatives

The closest relatives of the spikefish are the triplespines (family Triacanthidae), so named because they have a prominent spine at the front of the dorsal fin and two powerful pelvic spines—one on each pelvic fin. Such a three-spined arrangement is also responsible for their alternative name of tripodfish.

Unlike their close relatives the spikefish, all seven species of triplespines live in shallow water. The deepest-diving representative—the long-spined tripodfish (*Pseudotriacanthus strigilifer*) is found from surface brackish water habitats down to around 360 feet (110 m) in coastal waters. This means that the depth limit for this family only slightly overlaps what is the top end of the depth range for the spikefish.

Triplespines look a little like triggerfish and filefish, with a pointed head, eyes set well up on the skull, and distinctive dorsal and pelvic fin

spines. However, they do have characteristics of their own, like a long and narrow caudal peduncle and a deeply forked tail. Most species are found in sufficient numbers to support local fisheries. At least one—the short-nosed tripodfish (*Triacanthus biaculeatus*)—is used in traditional Chinese medicine.

## Size Range

In the spikefish family the smallest species, (*Atrophacanthus japonicus*), is only 2 inches (5 cm) long, while the biggest is a longsnout (*Halimochirurgus alcocki*) that is over four times that length—8.7 inches (22 cm).

Generally the tripodfish family members are bigger than their spikefish cousins, with the smallest—the longtail tripodfish (*Tripodichthys blochii*)—measuring 6 inches (15 cm) in length, while the largest are the blacktip tripodfish (*Trixiphichthys weberi*) and the short-nosed tripodfish, both growing to twice the length of the smallest at 12 inches (30 cm).

⬆ *The fleshy-lipped spikefish (*Tydemania navigatoris*) feeds by scraping the scales off other fish with its specially shaped teeth and jaws.*

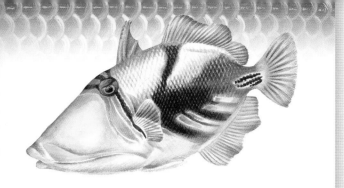

**Picasso triggerfish (*Rhinecanthus aculeatus*)**

**Common name** Triggerfish and filefish

**Families** Balistidae (triggerfish), Monacanthidae (filefish or leatherjackets)

**Order** Tetraodontiformes

**Number of species** Balistidae: 40 in about 11 genera; Monacanthidae: 104 in about 31 genera

**Size** From 1 in (2.5 cm) to 43.3 in (110 cm)

**Key features** Body usually compressed, roughly oval in shape; triggerfish body less deep, filefish covered in scales with several small spines on outer edge; mouth at tip of snout armed with powerful teeth; eyes set well back on head and toward top; 3 spines (2 in filefish) on first dorsal fin, last is very small; soft rays on second dorsal; well-formed caudal, often with extensions of topmost and lowermost rays; anal almost identical to second dorsal; pelvic fin has 1 spine and attached fold of skin; varied coloration: often spectacular, but sometimes unicolor in triggerfish

**Breeding** Eggs laid on site prepared by male; female triggerfish guard eggs, but males in filefish; some subtropical filefish release eggs in open water

**Diet** Sea urchins; also crustaceans (e.g., crabs), hard-shelled mollusks (e.g., snails), algae, worms, eggs, sea squirts, corals, zooplankton; also bottom-dwelling invertebrates (e.g., worms), moss animals (e.g., bryozoans), fish eggs, sea anemones, snails, slugs, and seaweed

**Habitat** Most species tropical or subtropical, but some extend into more temperate areas; frequently associated with coral reefs and shallow water, usually less than 165 ft (50 m) deep; some filefish prefer sandy or other fine-grained bottoms or seagrass meadows

**Distribution** Atlantic, Indian, and Pacific Oceans

⤴ *The 12-inch (30-cm) Picasso triggerfish (Rhinecanthus aculeatus) is commonly found in subtidal reef flats and shallow protected lagoons in the Indo-Pacific from the Red Sea down to South Africa and east to Hawaii.*

# Triggerfish and Filefish

Balistidae, Monacanthidae

*Eating sea urchins sounds pretty unsavory, as well as dangerous. Yet, that is what some triggerfish do, and without getting their eyes poked out in the process.*

TRIGGERFISH ARE SO NAMED BECAUSE of their dorsal fin-locking mechanism. The second (smaller) dorsal spine acts as a trigger, which "fires" the mechanism that firmly locks the larger first spine once it is raised in defense or alarm. The first spine and then the second are raised. Then a bony knob at the base of the second spine fits into a hollow at the bottom of the first to prevent the first spine from being lowered as long as this bony knob is lodged in position. The second spine can rotate within its base by a type of ball-and-socket joint arrangement— like people have in their hips. Filefish also have this same mechanism, which shows the close relationship between these two families.

## Triggers, Files, and Jackets

Another feature they share is the arrangement between pelvic bone, pelvic spines, and a fold of skin that lies between the pelvics and the anus. When the pelvic spine is raised, so is the skin flap, further emphasized by the pelvic bone rotating downward. The overall effect makes the triggerfish or filefish look larger, thus discouraging would-be predators.

These fish use such defense strategies if caught out in the open; but if close to a reef, they dive into the nearest crevice, raising their fins to lodge themselves inside. In this position the fish cannot be dislodged; when danger passes they lower their spines and swim away.

Both triggerfish and filefish have a third line of defense in the structure of their skin, which is usually covered in thick tough scales. In triggerfish the outer edge is rough, with one or more small spines, but in the filefish there are more spines, set closer together.

⊕ *These two colorful undulate triggerfish (Balistapus undulatus), swimming in coral reefs in the South Pacific, are searching for their favorite food—sea urchins—but they also eat mollusks and crustaceans.*

# Harmless Filefish or Toxic Puffer?

*C*anthigaster valentini* is an attractive Indo-Pacific fish that grows to around 8 inches (20 cm). It has four dark-brown bands that saddle its back, light-brown spots between the bands, and a creamy-white base body color. Its yellowish fins and blue streaks make it an extremely beautiful, boldly patterned fish.

*Paraluteres prionurus*, another Indo-Pacific species, also has four dark-brown bands, two of which saddle the back, plus yellowish fins and light-brown body spots. It grows to around 4.3 inches (11 cm), and its overall shape is remarkably similar to that of *Canthigaster valentini*. However, both these almost-identical replicas belong to totally separate families—*Canthigaster valentini* is Valentinni's sharpnose puffer (family Tetraodontidae), while *Paraluteres prionurus* is the black-saddled filefish (family Monacanthidae).

There are also other differences between these two lookalikes—the filefish is totally harmless, while the puffer is highly toxic. This is a prime example of how valuable close mimicry can be as a defense mechanism for the filefish.

The black-saddled puffer generally occurs in shoals numbering 100 individuals or more. On closer examination, though, as many as five of them are not puffers at all but black-saddled filefish. They "lose themselves" among the shoal and thus obtain protection from the reputation of the poisonous puffers that they mimic, since most predators will actively avoid attacking the puffers.

While these scales can give the skin a satin or velvet affect to the touch, they actually produce a rough sandpaperlike or filelike feel, especially when rubbed in a tail-to-head direction—hence the common name for these fish. Filefish are also called leatherjackets because of their thick skin. It generally feels smooth if rubbed in a head-to-tail direction, particularly in species that have no scales, like the beaked, long-nosed, or harlequin filefish (*Oxymonacanthus longirostris*).

## Popular Aquarium Fish

Despite their fame as sea-urchin crunchers, triggerfish also feed on other invertebrates, including crustaceans, like crabs, shrimp, and lobsters, as well as hard-shelled mollusks, like snails and clams. Different species of triggerfish will also eat algae (seaweed), worms, eggs, corals, sea squirts, and zooplankton, but their preference is for sea urchins.

Triggerfish are generally not fussy feeders. This adaptability, plus their interesting shapes

⬷ *A highly specialized feeder, the long-nosed filefish (Oxymonacanthus longirostris)—also known as the beaked or harlequin filefish—eats only the polyps of Acropora corals.*

can be comfortably maintained in aquaria for several years.

The same cannot be said of the black or red-toothed trigger (*Odonus niger*) from the Indo-Pacific and Red Sea, an elegant (but not black) species; it can vary its coloration from green to blue almost on a daily basis. It is easy to keep and feed, but because of its 20-inch (50-cm) size, it is challenging. The same is true for the similarly sized black-finned trigger (*Melichthys niger*) from the Indo-Pacific and the queen triggerfish (*Balistes vetula*) from the tropical west Atlantic—all spectacular fish that can challenge the best of aquarium keepers.

and beautiful colors, has made the species popular with aquarists despite some triggerfish being quite aggressive.

The most popular aquarium fish is the spectacular Picasso trigger (*Rhinecanthus aculeatus*)—also called the blackbar, whitebar, white-banded, or painted triggerfish—from the Indo-Pacific. Its very similar but more lightly patterned relative—the Arabian Picassofish or triggerfish (*R. assasi*), which is found in the Red Sea, Gulf of Oman, and Persian Gulf—is equally sought after, but it is more rarely seen.

Perhaps the most stunning aquarium species, though, may be the clown trigger (*Balistoides conspicillum*), an aggressive species from the Indo-Pacific; so too is the beautiful undulate, orange-green, orange-lined, or red-lined trigger (*Balistapus undulatus*), also from the Indo-Pacific.

With the exception of the clown trigger, which can grow to around 20 inches (50 cm) in length, the other three are modestly sized species that grow to a maximum length of 12 inches (30 cm) . Since many specimens are smaller than this, especially in captivity, and since most are sold at a size of around 4 inches (10 cm) or smaller, these attractive triggerfish

# The Urchin Crunchers

Triggerfish are renowned for their love of sea urchins. The fact is that while sea urchins look unpalatable with their hard shell and formidable spines, they do have a very tasty and succulent interior. The problem is how to get past their often poisonous defenses and gain access to the soft, juicy "meat" inside.

As in every case in which there is a challenge, evolution has equipped the triggerfish to enable it to tackle this tricky meal.

First, the triggerfish has a distinctive long, tapering head with the eyes set well back and near the top of the skull. It also has strong jaws and teeth. The positioning of the eyes allows triggerfish to grab hold of sea urchins by their spines without running the risk of injury to these vital organs. They can, therefore, repeatedly lift and drop a sea urchin onto the bottom, eventually resulting in the underside of the urchin being exposed. At this point the trigger will dive in among the shorter spines on the urchin's underbelly and tear open a hole with its powerful teeth. Usually the point of attack is the urchin's mouth; but once a hole has been created, the whole skeleton can be ripped to pieces, revealing the insides of the urchin.

Some triggerfish can also blow strong currents of water at a sea urchin until it blows it over, exposing the urchin to attack. This strategy is particularly useful when hunting long-spined sea urchins, like the various *Diadema* species.

# Chameleonlike Triggers

**C**hameleons are famous for their remarkable ability to match their surroundings and "disappear" from view. They are also well known for their unusual eyes, especially for their amazing ability to move their eyes independently of each other—enabling them to look forward and backward at the same time.

Triggerfish do not change color, at least not in the way that chameleons do. However, like chameleons, they do have the ability to rotate their eyes independently of each other. Quite what purpose this serves in triggerfish is not totally clear, but such sophisticated features generally give their owners some distinct advantage. Triggers are no exception, and their independent eye control probably allows them to keep one eye on their potentially dangerous food while the other eye keeps watch for dangerous enemies.

**The Long and the Short**

In the family Balistidae triggerfish can be as tiny as 3.8 inches (9.6 cm)—the outrigger triggerfish (*Xenobalistes punctatus*)—to the longest: the 40-inch (100-cm) stone trigger (*Pseudobalistes naufragium*).

The smallest in the family Monacanthidae is the diamond leatherjacket (*Rudarius exelsus*) at 1 inch (2.5-cm), while the 43.3-inch (110-cm) scrawled filefish (*Aluterus scriptus*) is longest.

Such factors make this species extremely challenging to keep in captivity for any length of time. Other species are relatively easy to feed once they have become used to aquarium life. Filefish have become very popular in aquaria, where their peaceful nature, interesting shapes, and body colors make such fascinating subjects.

## Grunting Fish

Both filefish and triggers are among a wide range of fish that can produce sounds. The sounds serve many purposes, from straightforward communication between individuals so they can keep in touch with each other and not stray too far from the shoal, to warnings between rivals (usually males) or possible predators.

In filefish and triggerfish sounds are produced in a variety of ways. For example, the spines of the dorsal, anal, pectoral, or pelvic fins are all used to generate sounds through stridulation (rubbing two bones together). In the painted or Picasso triggerfish the sound can come from rubbing the bones of the "arch" that supports the pectoral fins. This sound is amplified by the vibrations, which the stridulating pectoral arch, in turn, causes within the swim bladder. The sound produced is like the rapid beating of a drum or, more colorfully, the grunting of a pig.

Indeed, this strange sound is reflected in part of the Hawaiian name for both the painted triggerfish and the wedge-tailed triggerfish (*R. rectangulus*)—*humuhumu-nukunuku-a-pua'a*. The first half means "to stitch pieces together" and is possibly a reference to the sharp demarcation lines between the different straight-edged patches of color on the body that give the impression that they have been sewn together. The second half of the word loosely translates as "grunts like a pig."

Some of the filefish and triggerfish species can also produce quite loud grunting sounds, by grinding their jaw or pharyngeal (throat) teeth together. In some filefish there are even ridges on the back of their front teeth that are used to generate other strange sounds.

### Fine Feeders

Filefish do not tackle food that can "bite back" as triggers do in feeding on sea urchins and crustaceans, which can give their attacker a nasty nip. They tend to feed on small, bottom-living invertebrates (including worms), moss animals (bryozoans), and sea anemones. Some eat seaweeds and seagrasses, while others—like the black-saddled filefish—feed on fish eggs, snails, or sea slugs.

A few are highly specialized feeders. For example, the beaked, long-nosed, or harlequin filefish eats exclusively coral polyps (soft tissue of hard corals)—in fact, it is so specialized that it only feeds on polyps of *Acropora* corals.

⬆ *Usually it is the female triggerfish that do guard duty. In these waters off Borneo a clown triggerfish (Balistoides conspicillum) is protecting its eggs.*

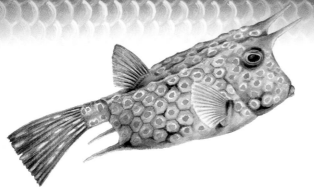

Longhorn cowfish (*Lactoria cornuta*)

**Common name** Boxfish and cowfish

**Family**       Ostraciidae (sometimes called Ostraciontidae)

**Subfamilies** Aracaninae, Ostraciinae

**Order**        Tetraodontiformes

**Number of species** 37 in 12 genera

**Size**         4.3 in (11 cm) to 21.7 in (55 cm)

**Key features** Body cubical or slightly longer and angular, encased in bony carapace or "shell" covered in thin, fleshy tissue; mouth small and partly beaklike; forehead may have hornlike projections; eyes located high on head; single dorsal fin placed well back on body, lacks hard spines; no pelvic skeleton or pelvic fins; coloration extremely variable and often bright: ranging from almost yellow all over to green with blue spots to deep-based colors highlighted with light spots

**Breeding**     Most species have harem system of single male and several females; eggs released into water (often at dusk) and abandoned; hatching takes about 2 days

**Diet**         Bottom-living invertebrates; also seagrasses

**Habitat**      Mainly shallow-water reefs; some species found in seagrass meadows or sand, rocks, or rubble; Aracaninae members prefer deeper waters down to 660 ft (200 m)

**Distribution** Tropical, subtropical, and sometimes temperate regions of Atlantic, Indian, and Pacific Oceans

⬆ *The 18-inch (46-cm) longhorn cowfish (*Lactoria cornuta*) is found in the Red Sea east to Polynesia and north to Japan. It inhabits weedy areas near rocks or reefs at depths of between 60 and 330 feet (18–100 m).*

# Boxfish and Cowfish

Ostraciidae

*Boxfish and cowfish have some odd characteristics, with rigid, boxlike bodies and often horns attached. They also have a built-in ability to poison themselves.*

THE BOXFISH AND COWFISH, ALONG with trunkfish, turretfish, and basketfish, form the family Ostraciidae. Strictly marine fish, they are most frequently encountered on shallow, tropical coral reefs, rubble areas, and seagrass meadows. Not all species are tropical or subtropical; the 8-inch (20-cm) striped cowfish (*Aracana aurita*) from southern Australian waters and the smaller *Kentrocapros aculeatus* from the western North Pacific are found in temperate waters down to 655 feet (200 m). The latter species, occurring at depths between 330 and 655 feet (100–200m), is therefore a strictly cold-water species.

## Food Fish with a Health Warning

Some larger boxfish are excellent food fish, although several have been linked to ciguatera poisoning, caused by eating contaminated fish. Every year around 50,000 people are affected by severe digestive system problems, but the death rate is very low (less than 1 percent).

## Comical Creatures

Most boxfish and cowfish attract interest because of their coloration, unusual body features (such as unfishlike "horns"), rigid boxlike body, and "comical" swimming style— all perfectly normal if you are a boxfish.

This comical effect is caused by restrictions enforced on the fish by their hard, inflexible body armor that does not let them bend or use their tail to propel themselves forward, as other fish do. Instead, they swim with their unpaired dorsal and anal fins, use their pectoral fins to balance themselves (they have no pelvic fins), and steer with their maneuverable tail.

⊙ *The hornlike projections and brightly colored scales of this longhorn cowfish (Lactoria cornuta) make it an attractive fish for the home aquarist, but at 18 inches (45 cm) in length it may grow too large for the tank.*

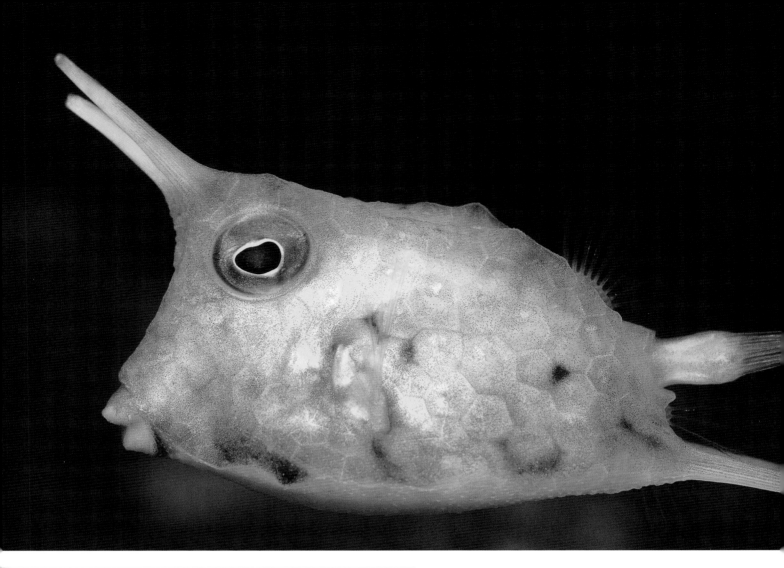

## Toxic Boxes

Boxfish and their relatives are popular among aquarists because of their swimming style and shapes. But species like the longhorn cowfish (*Lactoria cornuta*), the yellow, black-spotted, polkadot, or cube boxfish (*Ostracion cubicus*), and the spotted, white-spotted, blue-spotted, or Pacific boxfish (*O. meleagris*) all grow too large, from 10 to 18 inches (25–45 cm).

More dramatically, they release a toxin (ostracitoxin) into the water if they are alarmed. In the wild this poison is unpleasant for other fish and, at worst, lethal—not even the boxfish themselves are immune. On a reef it can defend itself with this poison and can swim away, but in an aquarium the toxins can kill not only the other tank occupants but themselves as well.

⊖ *A spotted boxfish (Ostracion meleagris) can defend itself by releasing toxins into the water as a deterrent.*

**Valentinni's sharpnose puffer (*Canthigaster valentini*)**

**Common name** Puffers and porcupinefish

**Families**    Triodontidae (three-toothed puffer or pursefish),
Tetraodontidae (puffers), Diodontidae
(porcupinefish or burrfish)

**Subfamilies** Tetraodontidae: Tetraodontinae, Canthigastrinae

**Order**      Tetraodontiformes

**Number of species** Triodontidae: 1 in 1 genus;
Tetraodontidae: 176 in 27 genera;
Diodontidae: 20 in 7 genera

**Size**       From 1.6 in (4 cm) to 48 in (1.2 m)

**Key features** Body elongated, almost spherical if inflated;
roundly pointed snout, mouth at tip; fused jaw
teeth project into beaklike structure: 2 fused
teeth (porcupinefish), 3 (three-toothed puffer), 4
(other puffers); eyes high on head; body scaleless
or short, pricklelike scales along belly (puffers),
sharp spines (porcupinefish); belly with large
purselike sac (three-toothed puffer); dorsal and
anal fins set well back on body; no pelvic fins;
coloration: variable, often brilliant, with spots
and patches (puffers); belly "purse" has yellow
ring circling prominent black "eye spot"; darker
and lighter shades of brown (porcupinefish)

**Breeding**   Spawn in groups in shallow nests in shallow
beach areas after new and full moon; freshwater
species spawn in pairs, male guards eggs or fry;
eggs hatch in under 2 days or up to a month
depending on species; planktonic larvae

**Diet**       Invertebrates; also sea urchins, starfish, soft-
bodied invertebrates, or other fish, and plants

**Habitat**    Mostly marine: tropical or subtropical; or fresh
brackish water; fine-grained to rocky bottoms;
shallow water down to 1,000 ft (300 m)

**Distribution** Atlantic, Indian, and Pacific Oceans

**Status**     World Conservation Union lists blunthead puffer
(*Sphoeroides pachygaster*) and Rapa sharpnose
puffer (*Canthigaster rapaensis*) as Vulnerable

⊕ *This 4.3-inch (11-cm) Valentinni's sharpnose puffer*
*(*Canthigaster valentini*) lives among coral in lagoons and reefs.*

# Puffers and Porcupinefish

Triodontidae, Tetraodontidae, Diodontidae

*When under attack, a puffer will inflate itself, making
it extremely hard to swallow. The porcupinefish can do
the same, but it is also covered in spines, making it an
even more awkward mouthful.*

THE PUFFERS AND PORCUPINEFISH, OR BURRFISH, are a
group of nearly 200 species that belong to
three closely related families—Diotontidae,
Triodontidae, and Tetraoclontidae—which easily
can be separated on the basis of their teeth.

## A Question of Teeth

The Diodontidae have two fused jaw teeth
("di" means two), the Triodontidae three ("tri"),
and the Tetraodontidae have four ("tetra").

The teeth of all families form a beaklike
structure—a single fused tooth in the upper jaw
and one in the lower jaw for porcupinefish
(*Diodon* species); two fused teeth in the upper
jaw separated by a suture (groove) in the three-
toothed puffer (*Triodon macropterus*); and two
fused teeth in each jaw, separated by a central
suture in other puffers (family Tetraodontidae).

## Dangerous Delicacies

In Japan there are establishments, called Fugu
Restaurants, that specialize in pufferfish cuisine.
Large specimens are easily filleted because the
fish have certain bones reduced or lacking
(especially in four-toothed puffers), no pelvic
girdle or fin, and their tasty flesh is very popular.

The restaurants (under license and closely
supervised) specialize in one of the 21 species in
the genus *Takifugu*. Monitoring is necessary
because puffers' internal organs are poisonous,
containing a toxin (tetraodotoxin) that can
either produce a druglike "high" but is not
life-threatening (as in *Takifugu* species) or, in
some other puffers, can actually kill people.

⊝ *Parts of the Fugu*
*puffer (*Takifugu*
*niphobles*), such as*
*the gonads and other*
*viscera, are poisonous,*
*but the fish is still used*
*in the preparation of*
*Japanese sushi.*

Tissues that are toxic can vary from species to species—for example, the skin, flesh, and testes of the torafugu or tiger puffer (*Takifugu rubripes*) are not poisonous, but its intestines, liver, and ovaries are. The smooth puffer's (*Lagocephalus laevigatus*) internal organs and skin are very toxic, as are the gut and muscles of the green puffer (*Tetraodon fluviatilis*).

However, the three-toothed puffer, the sharpnose puffer (*Canthigaster rostrata*), the eyespot or figure-of-eight puffer (*Tetraodon biocellatus*), and many porcupinefish are safe to eat; but the longspine porcupinefish (*Diodon holocanthus*) can cause "ciguatera" poisoning. In this case the fish itself is not toxic (as in tetraodotoxin poisoning) but becomes so if it eats fish or organisms that contain ciguatoxin. Thus it becomes a "carrier" of this poison.

The poisoning process begins at the bottom of the food chain when plant-eating fish eat algae containing ciguatoxin, acquiring some toxin in their tissues and passing it on when they are eaten by fish-eating predators, and so on. At every "link" in the food chain the concentration of ciguatoxin increases.

When people eat a ciguatoxin-containing fish, they have a high chance (73–100 percent) of being poisoned. In severe cases victims can die—fatalities range from 0.1 to 12 percent. In certain regions of the world the death rate is closer to 1 percent.

Species such as groupers (family Serranidae), moray eels (family Muraenidae), snappers (family Lutjanidae), and barracuda (family Sphyraenidae) are other fish that can also cause ciguatera poisoning.

⊕ *If threatened, this blotched porcupinefish (Diodon liturosus) takes large gulps of water into its intestines. In a few seconds its body inflates until it is spherical, many times the original size, causing its spines to stand on end—an unwelcome mouthful for any predator.*

## Aquarium Favorites

The beaklike teeth of puffers and porcupinefish are linked to powerful jaw muscles that can act as an efficient crushing tool. In terms of their day-to-day survival the beak allows puffers to tackle tough-shelled foods such as snails, other mollusks, and crustaceans.

In species like the figure-of-eight puffer, the freshwater or giant puffer (*Tetraodon mbu*), and the green puffer their appetite for snails is used by aquarists to clear tanks of snail infestations.

However, their slow, unusual swimming movements, "dumpy" body shape, large eyes, and attractive body patterns make some puffer species popular among aquarists, such as the Malabar puffer (*Carinotetraodon travancoricus*). —the smallest puffer at 1.6 inches (4 cm)—the figure-of-eight puffer, the mosaic or ocellated puffer (*T. cutcutia*), the spotted Congo puffer (*T. schoutedeni*), and the red-bellied or redeye puffer (*C. lorteti*), ranging from 2.4 to 6 inches (6–15 cm) long. Even the giant puffer, growing to 26.4 inches (67 cm) in the wild, is popular.

Among marine species peaceful puffers like the sharpnose puffers (genus *Canthigaster*) and some *Arothron* species are popular. Sharpnoses are small (under 6 inches, 15 cm), but the clown toado (*C. callisterna*) exceeds 9 inches (23 cm). *Arothron* species are much larger; the more colorful ones, like the dogface or black-spotted puffer (*A. nigropunctatus*), guineafowl puffer (*A. meleagris*), and white-spotted puffer (*A. hispidus*), are "substantial"—13 inches (33 cm) for the dogface, 20 inches (50 cm) for the other two. The giant of all puffers, the starry puffer or toadfish (*A. stellatus*), is 48 inches (120 cm).

# Molas

Molidae

*Molas look unfinished, with no true tail fin, but they have existed for over 12 million years. These gentle giants enjoy cruising surface waters and "sunbathing."*

Ocean sunfish (*Mola mola*)

**Common names** Molas

**Family** Molidae

**Order** Tetraodontiformes

**Number of species** 4 in 3 genera

**Size** 40 in (1 m) to 11 ft (3.3 m)

**Key features** Scaleless body relatively compressed (i.e., flattened side to side), almost circular, but slightly elongated in some species; head rounded; small mouth with 2 fused jaw teeth; tiny nostrils on each side of head; eyes small; gill slits are small openings at base of pectoral fins; no pelvic fins or true caudal fin; dorsal and anal fins long and spineless; pseudo-tail formed from last rays of dorsal and anal fins; coloration: drab bluish-brown on back, fading to lighter shades down sides and along belly; brighter in some species

**Breeding** Vast numbers of small eggs produced, especially by large female *M. mola* (300 million or more); eggs and sperm scattered in open water, then abandoned; larvae with body spines that initially increase in number and are later absorbed

**Diet** Mainly jellyfish and other soft-bodied invertebrates; also crustaceans, sea urchins, fish, and seaweed

**Habitat** Open sea, usually close to surface; some species dive deeper, from 900 ft (300 m) down to 2,200 ft (760 m)

**Distribution** Tropical, subtropical, and warm temperate regions worldwide

⊕ *The 11-foot (3.3-m) ocean sunfish (Mola mola) drifts at the surface while lying on its side or swims upright with its dorsal fin projecting above the water. It is believed the mola is the heaviest bony fish, up to 5,070 lb (2,300 kg), and with the most eggs (300 million).*

APPEARANCES CAN BE DECEPTIVE. OTHERWISE molas (or ocean sunfish) would not have been swimming in prehistoric oceans, as their earliest fossils prove. What is important is not what the fish looks like but how well suited it is for survival in its natural element. In this molas score high.

## Tail of a Sunfish

When very young, during larval stages, four species, such as the slender sunfish (*Ranzania laevis*) and the ocean sunfish (*Mola mola*), have a true, though primitive, tail. As the fish develop to adulthood, the tail is absorbed and gradually replaced with a pseudo-tail (clavus).

The large dorsal and anal fins (located well back on the body), as well as the clavus, can propel the molas forward at some speed if necessary, although mostly they are used to move these large fish gently through the open ocean waters where they spend their lives.

## Giant "Puffers"

Ocean sunfish look very different from puffer-fish (families Triodontidae and Tetraodontidae) and porcupinefish (family Diodontidae). Yet they are related and belong to the same order—the Tetraodontiformes. The main characteristics that link them are their teeth and their larvae. For example, all have fused jaw teeth: two in the sunfish, two in the Diodontidae, three in the Triodontidae, and four in the Tetraodontidae.

In addition, the larvae show that they are related to the boxfish (family Ostraciidae). Mola larvae have spines on their bodies, the number increasing as the larvae develop. At an early stage they carry four body spines (also typical of puffers and porcupinefish). Later the number of spines increases, and they are distributed around the body (as in boxfish). As the larvae

 **SEE ALSO** Boxfish 11:106; Puffers and Porcupinefish 11:108

change into recognizable miniature sunfish, they leave their puffer-boxfish ancestry behind as they grow up to 11 feet (3.3 m) and weigh nearly 5,070 pounds (2,300 kg), like molas.

## Gentle Sunbathers

For all their size and weight, ocean sunfish are gentle creatures that spend much of their time slowly cruising the surface layers of the world's tropical, subtropical, and warm temperate oceans. Often they lie on their side, looking as if they are dead or dying. While that may be true for some older or injured specimens, this unusual behavior is also typical of perfectly healthy individuals. They create an impression that they are "sunbathing," which may be why all four species are called "sunfish."

Despite its tendency to swim close to the surface, the ocean sunfish (also called giant sunfish, mola ocean sunfish, or headfish) can dive to over 900 feet (300 m). The sharptail sunfish (*Masturus lanceolatus*) goes even deeper—down to 2,200 feet (670 m).

## Small Mouth

With its two fused teeth and small mouth the ocean sunfish feeds on jellyfish, free-swimming crustaceans, squid, mollusks, and plankton, as well as sea urchins and seaweed. The dwarf, slender, truncated sunfish (*Ranzania laevis*) eats mainly free-swimming crustaceans. In their turn juvenile ocean sunfish fall prey to larger fish and sea lions, while tuna (*Thunnus* species) and shark (class Chondrichthyes) eat larger molas.

# Glossary

Words in SMALL CAPITALS refer to other entries in the glossary.

**Abbreviated heterocercal** term used to describe a HETEROCERCAL TAIL in which the upper lobe is less extended than in a typical heterocercal tail

**Adaptation** features of an organism that adjust it to its environment; NATURAL SELECTION favors the survival of individuals whose adaptations fit them to their surroundings better than other individuals

**Adipose fin** fatty fin located behind rayed DORSAL FIN in some fish

**Adult** fully grown animal that has reached breeding age

**Agonistic** any activity, aggressive or submissive, related to fighting

**Air bladder** see SWIM BLADDER

**Ammocete larva** filter-feeding lamprey LARVA

**Ampullae of Lorenzini** jelly-filled tubes on the head of sharks and relatives; responsible for detecting weak electrical impulses

**Anadromous** term describing a SPECIES that spends part of its life in the sea and part in freshwater habitats

**Anal fin** FIN located near the anus

**Appendicula** outgrowths from the umbilical cord of some sharks; appendicula enhance an embryo's ability to absorb UTERINE MILK

**Aquatic** associated with, or living in, water

**Arborescent organ** treelike modifications of GILL tissues found in air-breathing species like walking catfish

**Atriopore** small aperture in lancelets corresponding to the atrial, or exhalant, SIPHON in sea squirts

**Barbel** whiskerlike, filamentous sensory growth on the jaws of some fish, including catfish

**Benthic** occurring, or living, on the bottom

**Brackish water** water that contains salt in sufficient quantities to distinguish it from fresh water but not enough to make it sea water; brackish water is found in estuaries, mangrove swamps, and other habitats where fresh water and sea water mix

**Branchiostegal rays** flattish, riblike bones located ventrally behind the GILL covers and making up the floor of the gill chamber

**Brood** offspring of a single birth or clutch of eggs

**Brood pouch** structure formed from FINS or plates of a parent fish in which fertilized eggs are placed to hatch safely

**Bubble nest** nest of bubbles that harbors eggs or offspring of some fish

**Camouflage** markings or features of a creature that aid concealment

**Carnivore** creature whose diet consists exclusively of other animals

**Cartilaginous** formed of cartilage

**Catadromous** term describing a SPECIES that migrates from fresh water to the sea for spawning

**Caudal fin** "tail" FIN

**Caudal peduncle** part of the body where the tail begins

**Caudodorsal** term describing an extension of the CAUDAL FIN onto the back of the body; this fin contains RAYS but no spines; caudodorsal fins are found in catfish of the family Plotosidae

**Cephalic shield** head shield formed by bony plates, as found in upside-down catfish

**Cephalofoil** term used to describe the "'hammer" of hammerhead sharks; thought to provide lift and maneuverability

**Cerebellum** part of the hindbrain involved in the coordinated activity of muscles, posture, and movement

**Cerebral hemispheres** pair of symmetrical, rounded, convoluted tissue masses that form the largest part of the brain in many organisms, e.g., mammals

**Chordata** PHYLUM of animals having a single, hollow dorsal nerve cord, a NOTOCHORD, GILL SLITS, and a postanal tail; some of these characteristics may only be present in the earliest stages of development

**Chromatophore** pigment-containing cell whose shape or color can be altered

**Chromosome** tiny, rod-shaped structure in the cell NUCLEUS; chromosomes contain DNA, which carries genetic information

**Cilium** (*pl.* **cilia**) tiny, hairlike structure growing out from the surface of some cells; cilia are capable of whiplike actions and can facilitate movement

**Cirrus** (*pl.* **cirri**) hairlike or tentaclelike growth, e.g., as found on the nostrils, supraorbital area, and nose in some blennies

**CITES** Convention on International Trade in Endangered Species; an agreement between nations that restricts international trade to permitted levels through licensing and administrative controls; rare animals and plants are assigned categories

**Claspers** structures between the PELVIC FINS of male cartilaginous fish that allow them to clasp a female during mating, and that facilitate the transfer of sperm

**Class** taxonomic level below PHYLUM and above ORDER

**Cloaca** single chamber into which anal, urinary, and genital ducts (canals) open

**Clone** identical cell or individual derived from a single cell, e.g., an egg

**Community** all the animals and plants that live together in a HABITAT

**Compressed** term used to describe a structure that is flattened from side to side

**Cone** cone-shaped light-sensitive cell in the retina of the eye; cones are particularly sensitive to colors (see ROD)

**Copepoda** subclass of small crustaceans, some of which are parasitic; copepods do not have a hard carapace (shell) but have a single, centrally placed eye

**Cosmoid scale** type of SCALE found in many fossil and some primitive fish

**Countershading** color distribution seen in many fish in which the back is darker than the belly

**Crepuscular** active at twilight

**Cryptic coloration** camouflage-type coloration that helps organisms blend in with their surroundings; some species are cryptically colored at all times, while others, e.g., many squirrelfish, are cryptic during the day and more brightly colored at night

**Ctenoid scale** similar to the CYCLOID SCALE but with a toothed posterior edge rather than a smooth or wavy (crenulated) one

**Cusp** point or prominence, often on a tooth

**Cycloid scale** thin, flexible overlapping scale, roughly the shape of a human finger nail, found in modern bony fish and the primitive bowfin (*Amia calva*); the front edge of each scale is embedded in a special pouch in the surface of the skin; the back edge is free and smooth or wavy (crenulated) but not toothed as in CTENOID SCALES

**Dendritic** finely branched

**Denticle** small, toothlike scale found in sharks and some of their closest relatives (SEE PLACOID SCALE)

**Depressed** term used to describe a structure that is flattened from top to bottom

**Detritus** debris consisting of fragments of dead plants and animals

**Dimorphism** existence of two distinct forms

**Dioecious** having separate sexes (see HERMAPHRODITE)

**Display** any fairly conspicuous pattern of behavior that conveys specific information to others, usually to members of the same species; often associated with "courtship" but also in other activities, e.g., threat displays

**Diurnal** active during the day

**DNA** (deoxyribonucleic acid) the substance that makes up the main part of the chromosomes of all living things; DNA is the carrier of genetic information

**Dorsal** relating to the upper surface

**Dorsal fin(s)** FIN(S) on the back of a fish

**Electrocyte** electricity-generating cell, usually consisting of a modified muscle cell

**Electroplaque** stack or column of ELECTROCYTES; also referred to as electroplates

**Endangered species** SPECIES whose POPULATION has fallen to such a low level that it is at risk of EXTINCTION

**Endemic** term used to describe a SPECIES that is found in just one country or area

**Endostyle** longitudinal mucus-secreting groove found in the pharynx of sea squirts and relatives, lancelets, and lamprey LARVAE

**Endothermic** term used to describe animals that can generate internal body heat, e.g., mammals, birds, and certain fish like large tunas or some species of sharks

**Erectile** capable of being raised

**Esca** modified fleshy tissue on the tip of the first RAY of the DORSAL FIN (ILICIUM) in marine anglerfish; the esca resembles a small piece of "bait" that, when waved in the water, attracts PREY toward the anglerfish

**Estivation** dormancy or torpor during summer periods of heat and drought

**Evolution** development of living things by gradual changes in their characteristics as a result of MUTATION

**Exotic** term used to describe a SPECIES that is found in locations outside its natural distribution range, usually as a result of intentional or accidental introduction

**Extant** term used to describe SPECIES that are still in existence

**Extinct** term used to describe SPECIES that are no longer in existence

**Extinction** complete dying out of a SPECIES

**Falcate** sickle-shaped, as in the PECTORAL FINS of thresher sharks

**Family** group of closely related SPECIES (e.g., piranhas) or a pair of fish and their offspring

**Fin** winglike or paddlelike organ attached to certain parts of the body of a fish or other aquatic animals and used for steering, locomotion, and balance

**Fontanel** space or gap between some bones of the skull

**Food chain** sequence in which one organism becomes food for another, which in turn is eaten by another

**Fry** young fish

**Fusiform** body shape that tapers at both ends, i.e., spindle shaped

**Ganoid scale** SCALE found in most extinct ray-finned fish (Actinopterygii) consisting of a thick enamel-like layer underlaid by a dentine layer and a basal bony layer

**Genus** (*pl.* **genera**) group of closely related SPECIES

**Gill** organ by which a fish absorbs dissolved oxygen from the water and gets rid of carbon dioxide

**Gill raker** bristlelike extensions on the gill arches of filter-feeding fish; used for trapping suspended food particles in the water as it passes from the mouth via the GILLS and, subsequently, to the exterior through the GILL SLITS

**Gill slit** slit between the GILLS that allows water through

**Gonopodium** modified ANAL FIN of male LIVEBEARERS used to inseminate females

**Habitat** place where an animal or plant lives

**Harem** breeding "unit" consisting of a single male and several females, as in boxfish

**Hemoglobin** pigment that gives blood its red color; hemoglobin is used to carry oxygen around the body

**Herbivore** animal whose diet consists exclusively of plants

**Hermaphrodite** organism having both male and female reproductive organs

**Heterocercal** term used to describe a tail (CAUDAL FIN) in which the upper lobe contains the tip of the vertebral column (backbone); in such fins the upper lobe is usually considerably larger than the lower lobe

**Holotype** specimen on which the scientific description of a SPECIES is based; also referred to as the TYPE SPECIMEN

**Hybrid** offspring of a mating between two different SPECIES

**Hydrostatic organ** organ used in controlling flotation or buoyancy

**Hypertrophy** excessive growth as a result of an increase in cell size

**Hypocercal** term used to describe a tail (CAUDAL FIN) in which the lower lobe contains the end tip of the NOTOCHORD; in such fins the ventral (lower) lobe is usually larger than the dorsal (upper) one

**Ichthyologist** scientist specializing in the study of fish

**Ilicium** first modified ray of the DORSAL FIN in marine anglerfish, usually located on top of the head and bearing a fleshy tip (ESCA) used to lure unsuspecting victims toward the waiting anglerfish

**Inferior mouth** mouth located below the snout

**Interoperculum** bone joined anteriorly to the preoperculum and posteriorly to the interoperculum ligament, which, in turn, is connected to the OPERCULUM (gill cover)

**Introduced** describes a species that has been brought from places where it occurs naturally to places where it has not previously occurred

**Invertebrate** general term used to describe an animal that lacks a backbone

**IUCN** International Union for the Conservation of Nature, responsible for assigning animals and plants to internationally agreed categories of rarity (see table beow)

**Juvenile** young animal that has not reached breeding age

**Krill** tiny, shrimplike crustacean

**Labyrinth organ** respiratory organ found in gouramis and their relatives; formed from modified GILLS and housed in a chamber in the top of the gill cavity

**Larva** first stage of some fish SPECIES; newly hatched INVERTEBRATE

**Lateral** relating to the sides

**Lateral line organ** series of small fluid-filled pits linked to tubes that, in turn, are linked to a common canal; the lateral line detects movements (vibrations) in the water

**Leptocephalus** elongate, highly compressed, ribbonlike LARVAL stage of some fish such as eels

**Livebearer** SPECIES in which males introduce sperm into the body of the female, resulting in internal fertilization; developing embryos are generally retained by the female until birth

**Macula neglecta** part of the inner ear of sharks and related fish; important in sound perception

**Melanoblast** cell in which melanin (dark pigment) is formed

**Mermaid's purse** term used to describe the hard, leathery egg cases of sharks, skates, and rays

**Metamorphosis** changes undergone by an animal as it develops from the embryonic to the ADULT stage

**Microphthalmic** having tiny eyes

**Migration** movement of animals from one part of the world to another at different times of year to reach food or find a place to breed

**Milt** fluid containing male sperm

**Monotype** sole member of a GENUS

**Monotypic** GENUS or FAMILY that contains a single SPECIES

**Mouthbrooder** SPECIES in which the eggs are incubated in the mouth of one or other of the parents, according to species; FRY may also be protected this way

**Mutation** change in the genetic material (DNA) that, in turn, results in a change in a particular characteristic of an individual cell or organism

**Nape** the back of the neck

**Naris** (pl. **nares**) alternative word for nostril(s)

**Nasopharyngeal duct** nasal opening (nostril) in hagfish; also called the nasohypophysial opening

**Natural selection** process whereby individuals with the most appropriate ADAPTATIONS survive to produce offspring

**Nematocyst** stinging cell of sea anemones, jellyfish, and their relatives

**Neoteny** retention of larval characteristics into the sexually mature adult stage

**Neural spine** bone extension on the upper (dorsal) surface of individual vertebrae (back bones)

**Niche** part of a HABITAT occupied by a SPECIES, defined in terms of all aspects of its lifestyle (e.g., food, competitors, PREDATORS, and other resource requirements)

**Nocturnal** active at night

**Notochord** "rod" of cells along the back during the early stages of embryonic development in chordates; the notochord is replaced by the spinal column in all but the most primitive chordates

**Nucleus** dark, dense structure found in living cells of higher animals and plants, e.g., not in bacteria; the nucleus contains the CHROMOSOMES, which, in turn, contain genetic information in the form of DNA

**Nuptial tubercle** small, whitish, pimplelike growth developed by males during the breeding season, usually on the snout, head, cheeks and PECTORAL FINS; nuptial tubercles are known in at least 25 families of fish

**Olfactory** relating to the sense of smell

**Olfactory bulb** outgrowth from part of the lower anterior margin of the brain; responsible for detecting smells; also known as the OLFACTORY LOBE

**Olfactory lobe** see OLFACTORY BULB

**Olfactory sac** highly folded "chamber" in front of the OLFACTORY BULB; sensitive to smells

**Omnivore** animal whose diet includes both animals and plants

**Operculum** bone forming the gill cover in fish

**Orbital** relating to the eyes

**Order** level of taxonomic ranking

**Organ of Hunter** organ consisting of ELECTROCYTES that generate powerful electric pulses

**Organ of Sachs** organ consisting of ELECTROCYTES that are capable of generating weak electric pulses

**Osmoregulation** control of water balance in the body

**Osmosis** passage of molecules from a less concentrated to a more concentrated solution through a semipermeable membrane

**Otolith** grain of calcium carbonate in the semicircular canals of the ear; vital for balance

**Oviparity** egg laying; eggs and sperm are usually released into the environment where external fertilization takes place; in sharks the term is retained, although fertilization is internal

**Ovipositor** breeding tube extended by a female to place her eggs in a precise location

**Palate** roof of the mouth

**Papilla** (pl. **papillae**) small, usually cone-shaped projection

**Parallel evolution** development of similarities in separate but related evolutionary lineages through the operation of similar selective factors

**Parasite** organism that derives its food, for part or the whole of its life, from another living organism (belonging to a different SPECIES); parasites usually harm the organism on which they feed (the host)

**Parasphenoid** long, ridgelike bone with two side "arms"; located on the underside of the skull, this bone forms the "crucifix" in the crucifix fish (Arius spp.)

**Pectoral fin** one of the paired FINS connected to the pectoral girdle

**Pelvic fin** one of the paired FINS connected to the pelvic girdle

**Pharyngeal slit** alternative term for GILL SLIT

**Pharyngeal teeth** teeth located in the throat area and used primarily for grinding or crushing food

**Pheromone** substance released in tiny quantities by an animal and detected by another of the same SPECIES

**Photophore** luminous organ possessed by many deepwater bony and cartilaginous fish

**Phylum** (pl. **phyla**) group of animals whose basic or general plan is

## IUCN CATEGORIES

**EX** **Extinct**, when there is no reasonable doubt that the last individual of a species has died.

**EW** **Extinct in the Wild**, when a species is known only to survive in captivity or as a naturalized population well outside the past range.

**CR** **Critically Endangered**, when a species is facing an extremely high risk of extinction in the wild in the immediate future.

**EN** **Endangered**, when a species faces a very high risk of extinction in the wild in the near future.

**VU** **Vulnerable**, when a species faces a high risk of extinction in the wild in the medium-term future.

**LR** **Lower Risk**, when a species has been evaluated and does not satisfy the criteria for CR, EN, or VU.

**DD** **Data Deficient**, when there is not enough information about a species to assess the risk of extinction.

**NE** **Not Evaluated**, species that have not been assessed by the IUCN criteria.

similar, and which share an evolutionary relationship, e.g., the Chordata

**Phytoplankton** see PLANKTON

**Piscivore** animal whose diet consists exclusively of fish

**Placenta** spongy, blood-rich tissue found in mammals and some fish, such as livebearing sharks, by which oxygen and nutrients are supplied to—and waste products are removed from—embryos during development

**Placoid scale** small toothlike SCALE, often referred to as a DENTICLE, found in sharks; it consists of a bonelike basal part embedded in the skin and a backward-directed free, pointed border or spine covered in an enamel-like substance; placoid scales do not increase in size as the shark grows: instead, they are replaced throughout life

**Plankton** term used to describe the generally minute animals (zooplankton) and plants (phytoplankton) that drift in marine and fresh water

**Plica** fold or wrinkle, e.g., on the skin or a membrane

**Poikilothermic** term used to describe animals whose body temperature matches that of the environment, e.g., most fish, amphibians, and reptiles; such animals are frequently—but inaccurately—referred to as cold-blooded

**Polyp** individual animal making up a colony, as in corals; polyps have a tubular body, usually topped by a tentacle-ringed mouth, giving the animal the appearance of a miniature sea anemone

**Polyploidy** process by which cells possess three or more full sets of chromosomes

**Population** distinct group of animals of the same SPECIES or all the animals of that species

**Postanal tail** tail whose base originates behind the anus

**Predator** animal that hunts and kills other animals for food

**Preoperculum** anterior bone of the gill cover

**Prey** animal hunted for food

**Proboscis** elongated trunklike snout or projection

**Protandrous hermaphrodite** hermaphrodite that goes through a male phase before becoming a female

**Protogynous hermaphrodite** hermaphrodite that goes through a female phase before becoming a male

**Protractile** describes any structure that can be lengthened by, e.g., being pushed out, as spiny-finned fish are able to do with their mouths

**Race** see SUBSPECIES

**Radial muscle** muscle associated with the FIN RAYS of the head (known as radials)

**Range** geographical area over which an organism is distributed

**Ray** small spine that acts as a support for the FIN membrane

**Recruitment** addition of new individuals to a population, usually by reproduction or by inward migration from another population

**Refractive index** degree by which light rays are "bent" as they pass from one medium to another, e.g., from air to water

**Rete mirabile** dense network of blood vessels found in certain animals; heat exchange can occur between blood across this network allowing, e.g,. some sharks to retain body heat and maintain their internal temperature at a higher level than that of the surrounding water

**Retina** inner, light-sensitive layer of the eye on which images are formed

**Reverse countershading** type of color distribution seen in fish SPECIES that habitually swim upside down, e.g., some members of the Mochokidae; in these fish the belly is darker than the back, i.e., it shows the opposite color distribution found in normally COUNTERSHADED fish

**Rod** rod-shaped light-sensitive cell in the retina of the eye; rods are particularly sensitive to discerning shapes, especially in dim light (see CONE)

**Rostral** associated with a snout or ROSTRUM

**Rostrum** snout

**Rugosity** term used to describe rough or wrinkled tissue

**Scale** one of the usually tough, flattish plates that form part of the external covering of most fish species

**Scatophagous** term used to describe an animal that feeds on waste materials like sewage or feces; best-known fish exhibiting this trait are the scats

**Scute** platelike, modified scales found in some fish, including catfish

**Semicircular canal** fluid-filled canal in the inner ear; semicircular canals are set at right angles to each other, contain OTOLITHS, and are essential in maintaining body balance

**Shell gland** gland possessed by female sharks, skates, and rays; responsible for secreting the outer egg casing known as a MERMAID'S PURSE

**Siphon** funnel-shaped structure through which water can be taken in (inhalant) or discharged (exhalant)

**Spawn** eggs of a fish; the act of producing eggs

**Species** a POPULATION or series of populations that interbreed freely but not normally with those of other species

**Specific gravity** (**SG**) "weight," or density, of a liquid compared with pure water at 39.2° F (4° C); pure water has an SG value of 1.000, while the SG of seawater is around 1.020

**Spiracle** porelike opening associated with the GILLS

**Spiral valve** spiral infolding of the intestinal wall in primitive fish like sharks and rays

**Standard length** (**SL**) length of a fish measured from the tip of the snout to the CAUDAL PEDUNCLE

**Stridulation** vibration or rubbing together of two surfaces to produce a sound; in fish it usually refers to rubbing together of bones or fin spines, e.g., in some filefish and triggerfish

**Stripping** removal of eggs and sperm from ripe fish by the application of gentle pressure along the abdomen

**Suborbital** located under the orbit, or eye socket

**Subphylum** grouping of organisms sharing a number of characteristics in addition to those shared by members of a PHYLUM; examples of a subphylum are the sea squirts and relatives (Urochordata) and the backboned animals (VERTEBRATA), which together form the phylum CHORDATA

**Subspecies** subdivision of a SPECIES that is distinguishable from the rest of that species; often called a RACE

**Substrate** bottom of an aquatic HABITAT

**Subterminal** located underneath the end or tip, e.g., a subterminal mouth is one located underneath the tip of the snout

**Suprabranchial chamber** cavity or space above the gill chamber; the suprabranchial chamber houses the suprabranchial organ, i.e., modified gill tissues used by air-breathing fish, such as walking catfish

**Supraorbital** located above the orbit, or eye socket

**Suture** line along which two or more bones are immovably joined, as in the skull

**Swim bladder** gas-filled sac found in the body cavity of most bony fish; the amount of gas in the swim bladder can be regulated, allowing the fish to rise or sink in the water

**Symbiosis** relationship between two unrelated organisms from which both parties benefit, e.g., the light-producing bacteria that flashlight fish have in special cheek pouches (light organs); organisms that live in this manner are referred to as symbionts

**Symphysis** junction between the left and right sides of the jaw, i.e., where both bones meet and fuse at the front

**Tapetum lucidum** layer of light-reflecting tissue located under the retina; it amplifies the amount of light entering the eye and assists vision under poor light conditions

**Taxonomy** studying, naming, and grouping of living organisms; also termed classification

**Tendril** entwining, fiberlike extension on some shark and ray egg cases that allows the eggs to attach themselves to underwater objects like seaweeds

**Terminal** located at the end or tip, e.g., a terminal mouth is one located at the tip of the snout

**Territory** area that an animal or

animals consider their own and defend against others

**Thermocline** zone between warm surface water and colder deeper layers

**Tholichthys** term used to describe the young of certain fish, notably the scats, for a period after hatching; these larvae have large heads in relation to the body and protective bony plates and spines

**Thoracic** describes the area in or around the chest (thorax)

**Thunniform swimming** swimming technique in which the tail beats rapidly from side to side, but the body remains rigid; this type of swimming is found in tunas

**Tonic immobility** trancelike state or hypnosis exhibited by many animals, including some sharks and their relatives

**Total length** (**TL**) length of a fish measured from the tip of the snout to the tip of the CAUDAL FIN

**T-position** position adopted by at least some *Corydoras* species during mating, in which the female aligns herself at right angles to her mate's body, with her mouth close to his genital aperture

**Truncated** term often used to describe a CAUDAL FIN that has a straight, or more-or-less straight, edge

**Tubercle** small rounded swelling, nodule, or protuberance, as found, e.g., on the body of banjo catfish

**Type specimen** see HOLOTYPE

**Uterine milk** nutritious secretions produced in the womb (uterus) of female sharks during pregnancy; developing embryos feed on these secretions

**Uterus** womb

**Variety** occasional variation in a species not sufficiently persistent or geographically separate to form a SUBSPECIES

**Ventral** relating to the underside

**Vertebra** any of the bones of the spinal column

**Vertebrata** SUBPHYLUM of the PHYLUM Chordata characterized, especially, by a brain enclosed in a skull (cranium) and having a backbone (vertebral column) enclosing the spinal cord

**Viviparity** alternative term for LIVEBEARING

**Weberian apparatus** series of four small bones connecting the swim bladder to the ear in some fish (superorder Ostariophysi), including the catfish

**World Conservation Union** see IUCN

**Yolk sac** source of nourishment for some FRY prior to and immediately after hatching

**Zooplankton** see PLANKTON

# Further Reading

## General
Allen, G. R., **Freshwater Fishes of Australia**, T. F. H. Publications, Inc., Neptune City, NJ, 1989

Bond, C. E., **Biology of Fishes**, Saunders College Publishing, Philadelphia, PA, 1979

Campbell, A., and Dawes, J. (eds.), **The New Encyclopedia of Aquatic Life** Facts on File, New York, NY, 2004

Gilbert, C. R., and Williams, J. D., **National Audubon Society Field Guide to Fishes**, Alfred A. Knopf, New York, NY, 2002

Hayward, P., Nelson-Smith, T., and Sheilds, C., **Collins Pocket Guide to Sea Shore of Britain and Europe,** HarperCollins, London, U.K., 1996

Helfman, G. S., Collette, B. B., and Facey, D. E., **The Diversity of Fishes**, Blackwell Scientific Publications, Cambridge, MA, 1997

Meinkoth, N. A., **National Audubon Society Field Guide to North American Seashore Creatures**, Alfred A. Knopf, New York, NY, 1998

Moyle, P. B., and Cech, J. J. Jr., **Fishes: An Introduction to Ichthyology** (4th edn.), Prentice-Hall, Inc., Upper Saddle River, NJ, 2000

Nelson, J. S., **Fishes of the World** (3rd edn.), John Wiley and Sons, Inc., New York, NY, 1994

Page, L. M., and Burr, B. M., **A Field Guide to Freshwater Fishes (North America, North of Mexico)** (Peterson Field Guide Series), Houghton Mifflin Co., Boston, MA, 1991

Paxton, J. R., and Eschmeyer, W. N., **Encyclopedia of Fishes** (2nd edn.), Academic Press, San Diego, CA, 1998

Spotte, S., **Captive Seawater Fishes**, John Wiley & Sons, Inc., New York, NY, 1992

## Specific to this volume
Garrick-Maidment, N., **Seahorses: Management and Care**, Kingdom Books, Havant, U.K., 1997

Greenwood, P. H., **J. R. Norman: A History of Fishes**, Benn, London, U.K., 1975

Kuiter, R. H., **Seahorses, Pipefishes and their Relatives**, TMC Publishing, Chorleywood, U.K., 2000

Lourie, S. A., Vincent, A. C. J., and Hall, H. J., **Seahorses: An Identification Guide to the World's Species and Their Conservation**, Project Seahorse, London, U.K., 1999

Love, R. M., **Probably More Than You Want to Know about the Fishes of the Pacific Coast**, Really Big Press, Santa Barbara, CA, 1991

Wheeler, A., **The Pocket Guide to Freshwater Fishes of Britain and Europe**, Dragon's World, Limpsfield, U.K., 1992

Wheeler, A., **The Pocket Guide to Saltwater Fishes of Britain and Europe**, Dragon's World, Limpsfield, U.K., 1992

# Useful Websites

**http://www.fishbase.org/home.htm**
An amazing website full of information even on obscure fish

**http://www.si.edu/resource/faq/nmnh/fish.htm**
A useful list of alternative reference for all kinds of fish

**http://www.ucmp.berkeley.edu/vertebrates/basalfish/chondrintro.html**
Covers both fossil and living species, with good links

# Picture Credits

**Abbreviations** A Ardea, London; BCL Bruce Coleman Limited; FLPA Frank Lane Picture Agency; NHPA Natural History Photographic Agency; NPL Naturepl.com; P Photomax; P.com/OSF Photolibrary.com/Oxford Scientific Films;  SPL Science Photo Library
t = top; b = bottom; c = center; l = left; r = right

Jacket tl Gerard Lacz/FLPA;tr David Fleetham/P.com/OSF; bl Jeff Rotman/NPL; br Paul Kay/P.com/OSF

8 Max Gibbs/P; 10–11 Minden Pictures/FLPA; 14–15 Seapics.com; 17 Norbert Wu/P.com/OSF; 18–19 Max Gibbs/P; 20–21 Peter Scoones/NPL; 21 David Fleetham/P.com/OSF; 23 David Hall/NPL; 24 David Shale/NPL; 24–25 Pat Morris/A; 27 Constantinos Petrinos/NPL; 31t W. Wisniewski/FLPA; 30–31 David Fox/P.com/OSF; 32–33 P.com/OSF; 33 Paul Kay/P.com/OSF; 34 W. Wisniewski/FLPA; 37 Ron & Valerie Taylor/A; 39, 40 Max Gibbs/P; 40–41 Jurgen Freund/NPL; 42–43 Constantinos Petrinos/NPL; 44–45 Peter Scoones/NHP; 45b B.Jones & M. Shimlock/NHPA; 46 Jurgen Freund/NPL; 47 Clive Bromhall/P.com/OSF; 49, 51, 52–53 Max Gibbs/P; 55 Colin Marshall/FLPA; 56 Paul Kay/P.com/OSF; 58 Max Gibbs/P; 59 B. Jones & M. Shimlock/NHPA; 60 Constantinos Petrinos/NLP; 62 B. Jones & M. Shimlock/NHPA; 64–65 Max Gibbs/P; 66–67 Constantinos Petrinos/NPL; 69 David Fleetham/P.com/OSF; 70 Max Gibbs/P; 71 B. & P. Boyle/A; 73 Max Gibbs/P; 75 Doug Wechsler/NPL; 77 Roger Tidman/NHPA; 78 Rodger Jackman/P.com/OSF; 79 Paul Kay/P.com/OSF; 81 Rodger Jackman/P.com/OSF; 83 Pat Morris/A; 84–85 Jeff Rotman/NPL; 86–87, 88 Max Gibbs/P; 89 Florian Graner/NPL; 90–91 Roy Waller/NHPA; 93 Sue Daly/NPL; 94–95, 95t, 97 Max Gibbs/P; 101 Howard Hall/P.com/OSF; 102 Jurgen Freund/NPL; 103 David Fleetham/P.com/OSF; 104–105 Georgette Dowma/NPL; 107t, 107b Max Gibbs/P; 108–109 Karen Gowlett-Holmes/P.com/OSF; 109 Ken Lucas/A; 111 Richard Herrmann/P.com/OSF

Artists Denys Ovenden, Mick Loates, Colin Newman

# Set Index

A **bold** number shows the volume and is followed by the relevant page numbers (eg., **37**: 8, 70).

Common names in **bold** mean that the fish (e.g., **shark, great white**) or group or family of fish (e.g., **sheatfish**) has an illustrated main entry in the set. Underlined page numbers (e.g., **37**: 36–37) refer to the main entry for that fish or group.

*Italic* page numbers (e.g., **37**: 49) point to illustrations of fish in parts of the set other than the main entry.

Page numbers in parentheses—e.g., **34**: (87)—locate information in At-a-glance boxes.

Fish or families or groups of fish with main entries in the set are indexed under their common names, alternative common names, and scientific names.

**124**

**127**